Lighting

Lighting

Creative planning for successful lighting solutions

Elizabeth Wilhide

with photography by Ray Main

RYLAND
PETERS
& SMALL
LONDON NEW YORK

First published in the United States in 1998.
This revised edition published in 2004 by
Ryland Peters & Small, Inc
519 Broadway
5th Floor
New York NY 10012
www.rylandpeters.com

10 9 8 7 6 5 4 3 2 1

ISBN 1 84172 681 8

Printed and bound in China

For this edition:

Designer	**Sarah Fraser**
Senior editor	**Annabel Morgan**
Picture research	**Claire Hector**
Production	**Patricia Harrington**
Art director	**Gabriella Le Grazie**
Publishing director	**Alison Starling**
Illustrator	**John Woodcock**

*The publishers have made every effort to ensure that all
instructions given in this book regarding electrical installations are
accurate and safe, but they cannot accept liability for any resulting
injury, damage, or loss to person or property, whether direct or
consequential, and howsoever arising. The publishers recommend
that even the most minor electrical work is carried out by a
qualified electrician.*

Library of Congress Cataloging-in-Publication Data

Wilhide, Elizabeth.
  Lighting : creative planning for successful lighting solutions /
Elizabeth
Wilhide ; with photography by Ray Main.
     p. cm.
  Includes index.
  ISBN 1-84172-681-8
  1. Lighting, Architectural and decorative. 2. Interior decoration. I.
Main, Ray. II. Title.
  NK2115.5.L5W563 2004
  747'.92–dc22
                              2004003119

Contents

In the five years since the first publication of this book, the options available for home lighting have continued to broaden in scope. At the upper end of the market, classic modern lights by designers such as Achille Castiglioni, Tom Dixon, and Ingo Maurer are increasingly sought by those who furnish their homes with other similarly high-profile "designer" products. In the mainstream, playful forms of decorative light—such as strings of mini lights, light nets, and lava lamps—have never been more popular. At the cutting edge, contemporary artists and designers are redefining light as a sculptural medium, using LEDs and fiber optics, among other technological innovations, as well as exploring a host of new and often surprising materials.

For everyone, lighting remains one of the most critical factors in the way a home looks and works. From the welcoming porch light to the reassuring nightlight, from the kitchen spotlight to the angled desk lamp, we rely unthinkingly on lighting for efficiency, safety, and security in every sphere of our lives. Lighting is the practical adjunct without which everyday routines could not be performed without difficulty, or even a degree of danger.

Basic practicality, however, is only part of the story. No other single element in the interior repertoire has such power to affect one's sense of wellbeing. What good lighting provides is the mysterious X-factor that makes the difference between a room that is bland and dull and one that is sparking with life. Today, there is a greater appreciation than ever before of lighting's creative potential in generating that vital sense of mood and atmosphere.

We may be more familiar with the different types of light source available, from standard incandescent and fluorescent to the relative newcomer, halogen, but lighting in general is still often perceived as a difficult and complex area. For this reason, along with the fact that there is a tendency to choose lights based on the appearance of the fixture alone, the true potential of lighting can go unexplored. Choice of lighting ought to be one of the very first decisions that is taken when decorating a room. At the very least, it is important not to neglect simple alterations to existing lighting arrangements that can vastly improve the way space is perceived. Lighting is not merely about the style of fixtures; it concerns the color, direction, and intensity of light itself, from the intimate glow of a shaded table lamp, or the white sparkle of a low-voltage halogen spot, to the uplifting quality of subtly diffused light reflecting off walls and ceilings.

In this new and revised edition, we have taken the opportunity to include a substantial proportion of new images that reflect the way home lighting has evolved and will continue to develop. But the original purpose of the book remains the same: to demystify technicalities and introduce a wide range of inspirational ideas and practical strategies for bringing a new quality of light to your home.

Introduction

Decorating *with* light

The quality of the light around us has a profound effect on our emotional well-being that should not be underestimated. In practical terms, light defines space, enhances color, and reveals the intricacies of texture and form; in short, it makes our surroundings visible. But at the same time, light generates an almost indefinable sense of mood and atmosphere; it is the mysterious and almost imperceptible "X factor" in interior design.

Creating a successful lighting plan requires an understanding of the effect of different light sources, a working familiarity with the enormous choice of light fixtures and what they do and, last but not least, the practical common sense to choose the right fixture in any given context. This is what one might describe as the technical side of lighting design, and although it may appear superficially intimidating and complex, in reality it is not particularly difficult to master.

What is perhaps more important, however, is gaining an appreciation of the way light affects our lives. Decorating with light is less about selecting an attractive table lamp than learning to recognize the subtle ways in which lighting can make us not only comfortable and at ease in our surroundings but can also actively promote enjoyment and pleasure.

Thinking about light in this almost abstract sense—pinning down that elusive "X factor," in other words—means first going back to square one and analyzing exactly why and how we respond to different qualities of light. It means temporarily setting to one side considerations about style, function, and efficiency, and instead focusing on less tangible issues to do with the way that different types of light make us feel. The starting point for this process, understandably, is natural light, the rhythms and patterns of daylight to which, as human beings, we are naturally attuned.

Light is what we see by, but it is also what we feel by—it has an emotional as well as a practical role to play. The quality of light, whether it be natural or artificial, has a critical impact on mood and atmosphere. It can lift our spirits or depress us, excite us or soothe us, intimidate and alarm us or make us feel safe and secure. Before proceeding to consider the enormous variety of different fixtures, sources, and plans that can be used to light the home, it is worth first thinking about the types of natural and artificial light that are enjoyable and comfortable as well as the types that are not.

The feel-good factor

As humans, we are exceptionally light-sensitive creatures. Sight is our dominant sense, and through it we can appreciate minute variations in hue, tone, form, and movement. Compared to many other animals, which rely more acutely on hearing and smell, we enjoy a rich visual world full of subtlety and nuance. Light is the means by which such valuable distinctions are conveyed.

Natural light is the benchmark for all the artificial alternatives. What we instinctively enjoy about daylight is its variety. In different seasons, at different latitudes, at different times of the day, light is constantly changing. As weather systems develop and the sun rises and sets, light levels, colors, and directions alter, changing our perceptions of texture and form. The dappled mobile light of a shady summer garden, the brilliance of high noon beneath a cloudless Mediterranean sky, the rich, saturated colors of dusk or the pearly glow of dawn, each have their own sensual, atmospheric qualities. Think about a woodland walk, where sunny glades alternate with patches of deep shade and shafts of light penetrate the leafy forest canopy—or a stroll by the

sea, with light dancing and glinting on the surface of the water—or a hike over an open hillside as clouds scud across the sky, casting swiftly moving shadows on the ground.

If natural light can provide us with an instinctive appreciation of variety, it can also demonstrate how tedious and uncomfortable uniformity can be. Beneath a dull, gray overcast sky in a northern latitude, shadows are softer, form is indistinct, and color is more muted: life, in short, is less exciting, and the overall effect can be oppressive. At the opposite extreme, the unremitting glare of a harsh desert sun is brutally tiring and uncompromising.

Above: Light slanting through venetian blinds casts moody shadows. An artificial lighting plan should strive to create an equivalent richness and diversity of effect.

Left: A glass roof allows daylight to stream into the interior. At night, wall-mounted floodlights with barn-door attachments provide bright and focused illumination.

ways, artificial light can create and enhance a sense of occasion. Far from being second-rate substitutes for daylight, such lighting is theatrical, celebratory, and full of vitality.

It is equally simple to think of ways in which artificial light can be negatively employed. The blind terror of the interrogation cell is symbolized by the single bare light bulb glaring from the ceiling. The boredom of the waiting room is echoed in oppressive, diffused overhead lighting. The clinical nature of a hospital corridor is spelled out by cold strip lighting.

Recognizing the positive and negative associations of both natural and artificial light is an important step toward creating a good lighting plan in the home. When an interior seems to be uncomfortable, inhospitable, or lacking in atmosphere, and for no readily identifiable reason, all too often the lighting is at fault, replicating precisely those conditions we find most unsympathetic in the natural world. A bright unshielded bulb on a hanging cord over a dining table is equivalent to the bare bulb of the interrogator or the harsh midday sun; the dim overhead ceiling light in the living room duplicates the monotony of the waiting room or the tedium of a gray day; the flickering fluorescent in the kitchen is reminiscent of the sterile light of the laboratory or the bilious light of a thundery sky.

Our experience of light is not confined to the natural world. While electrical light is little more than a century old, human beings have lived with artificial light since the days when fires lit at the mouth of the cave kept darkness and marauding animals at bay. Many of these artificial sources have an inherent appeal of their own that is every bit as evocative as the effect of natural light. The homey flicker of firelight on a cold winter night, the warm intimacy of a candlelit dinner table, the festive charm of fairy lights or lanterns strung up in the trees around an outdoor taverna, the breathtaking magic of fireworks exploding in a dark sky, the grandeur of floodlit architectural monuments, the high drama of cinematic or stage lighting—in countless and diverse

Above: Candlelight is living, mobile light, warm and welcoming, flattering to the complexion, and instantly atmospheric. This pretty branched wall sconce with crystal drops has an abundance of period charm.

Right: A pair of lanterns diffuses soft candlelight; votive candles in glass containers are ranged along the windowsill.

Far right: Jasper Morrison's "Glo-ball" in its floor-standing version provides soft background illumination without overwhelming the warm, welcoming glow from the fireplace.

Above: A glassed-in walkway brings light into the heart of the home, dissolving the boundaries between inside and out.

Bad lighting makes us ill at ease in our surroundings. Conversely, sympathetic lighting enhances our perception of interior space. Rooms are alive with detail and color; texture and form gain definition; everyday activities are both practical and pleasurable.

Artificial light is often seen principally as a means to provide adequate illumination when natural light levels are low. But the aim of good lighting is not merely to enable us to see what we are doing once the sun goes down. It is to provide a richness of visual experience: both the subtlety and variety we enjoy in natural light, and the sparkling magic of light-filled celebrations.

Right: White and sparkling halogen lighting is the perfect complement to sleek, modern decor, enhancing the smooth, reflective finishes and generating a sense of spaciousness.

Natural light is the starting point for creating a lighting plan. Although we rely exclusively on artificial light after nightfall, in most homes, for much of the time, natural and artificial light must work in tandem. If the weather is bad, if we need to perform concentrated work, or if a room has a poor aspect, artificial lighting is needed to supplement natural light levels. Artificial lighting is also needed at transitional times, such as early morning or late afternoon. Assessing the type of natural light that a room receives with a view to enhancing its quality is an important first step when planning lighting.

Enhancing natural light

All "habitable" rooms should receive some direct daylight, which means they must be lit by at least one window. The exceptions are kitchens, bathrooms, and utility areas, which should have some ventilation but need not necessarily be furnished with windows. Unfortunately, legislation does not guarantee that the quality of natural light in a room is good, merely that daylight is present.

Orientation is a key factor in determining the quality of natural light. Two identically decorated rooms on the same level, but facing opposite directions, will appear very different due to the type of daylight they receive. A room receiving light from the north or northeast will always appear cooler and darker than a room with a southerly or southwesterly aspect. (For these purposes, the context is assumed to be the northern hemisphere; for the southern hemisphere, the orientation is reversed.)

North light is significantly cooler and whiter than the light cast from the south; it is also more even. For both of these reasons, a north-facing aspect has long been favored for artists' studios:

the coolness of north light renders colors more faithfully, in contrast to the rich, golden tones of light from the south, and its evenness provides relatively diffused and steady light levels rather than well-defined or lengthening shadows.

What is preferable for artists, however, may not be quite so sympathetic for everyday living. Human beings naturally gravitate toward sunny spots, seeking visual and physical warmth. Sunny, bright rooms are welcoming, cheerful, and full of vitality, while rooms that receive only indirect light can appear rather bland, chilly, and unfriendly.

Above: Soft cotton drapery filters natural light spilling in through the expanse of glazing. The diffusing effect is exactly the same as shading a light bulb.

Left: A ceiling recess provides a supremely discreet concealed source of light, equipped with a combination of 50-watt low-voltage downlights and a warm fluorescent strip.

You cannot alter the basic orientation of your home, but you can bear the aspect of each room in mind when it comes to the disposition of space. If your home provides the opportunity for flexible planning, choose the sunnier, south-facing rooms as locations for the kitchen, study, or main living areas, where you will necessarily spend more of your time during daylight hours. Rooms that are principally used after night has fallen, such as bedrooms, need not be so well aspected, since they will be experienced largely by artificial light.

In a similar way, if it is possible, it can sometimes make sense to turn the planning of your home upside down. Many houses, for example, have a level below ground where the kitchen and service rooms are located. Since the amount of light that a window admits depends on how much open sky is visible through the window, it is obvious that rooms that are situated on lower levels will tend to be darker. In the contemporary lifestyle, however, the kitchen is increasingly becoming a living area,

Right: A room with a dual aspect will have an infinitely better quality of light than one lit from one direction only, where contrasts of light and shade may be too great.

Below left: To increase light in a room, windows can easily be converted into glass doors by removing the windowsills and wall below.

Below and bottom right: Skylights add another dimension to an interior, leading the eye upwards and creating a sense of space.

where the entire family congregates, between as well as during mealtimes. If it is possible for you to move the kitchen up a floor into a position that enjoys higher levels of natural light, you will radically increase your enjoyment of the space, as well as improve its working practicality.

Increasing the size of the existing windows in your house is one obvious way of bringing more light into an interior. The simplest way of making a window larger is to lengthen it by dropping the sill and removing the area of solid wall below. This alteration has no structural implications and merely involves basic building work.

A rather more complicated alteration is to increase the size of the window by widening the opening, changing, for example, a sash window into french doors. This involves installing a compensating beam across the top of the new opening to bear the structural load from above. The same is true if you are creating a new window in a wall where none has existed previously.

The positioning of new windows is critical. A room lit by a single window will always have extremes of light and shade, ranging from very bright, well-lit areas in the vicinity of the window to deep shadow and dusky gloom at the opposite end of the room. If there is the opportunity, the solution to this problem is to make a new opening in a solid exterior wall, so that the room will then be lit by windows on two sides. Adding another window on a flanking wall will not only introduce more light *per se*, it will also improve the quality of light in the interior by reducing glare and strong contrast at the same time as introducing greater liveliness and variety of light throughout the day.

Above: A long, narrow sliver of window inset at the top of a wall provides tantalizing views from a staircase landing and introduces extra light into a potentially dark circulation space.

Size and number of windows have obvious implications for the amount and quality of natural light a room receives. Windows have increased dramatically in size over the centuries, following advances in construction methods and glass technology. While our ancestors had to be content with tiny casement openings filled with small, cloudy panes, we now have the technology to design and build entire houses of glass. In most homes, naturally enough, the reality lies somewhere between these two extremes.

Installing overhead windows, in the form of glass skylights, is another way of introducing a flood of light into dark and dim areas of the home. In addition to increasing the amount of natural light in an interior, skylights also create a feeling of spaciousness and expansion by leading the eye upward.

Natural light cannot be considered in isolation from decoration and furnishing. Pale walls, for example, will reflect available light and spread it around a room, while darker, more intensely colored surfaces are lightabsorbent and hence create darker surroundings with a greater sense of enclosure. Walls are not the only surface to take into account. White ceilings act as an enormous reflector for natural and artificial light, while white floors will increase the effect significantly. Colors from the warm end of the spectrum, such as yellows and creams, can take the chilliness out of north light, while cooler colors, such as blues and greens, look luminous and dazzling in direct sunlight. Texture also has an strong impact: matte surfaces reflect less light than those with a sheen, such as metal, glass, tile, and gloss paint.

Window treatments have an obvious and direct effect on the way natural light is perceived. Curtains and drapery that pull back from the window frame rather than overhang and obscure it allow as much light as possible to penetrate the interior. If privacy is important or views are less than welcome, translucent coverings such as fine cotton drapes or plain window shades have a soft and gentle diffusing effect. Just as a tinted shade will color the light from a table lamp, semitransparent colored fabric hanging at the windows will wash daylight with a subtle tone. Slatted wooden shutters, venetian blinds, gauze, and lace all filter light in various ways, creating evocative patterns that alter with the direction and level of the sun.

Above: Glass bricks make strong partition walls or internal space dividers, with the added advantage of maintaining interior views and spilling light from one area to another.

It is not always possible, however, to provide all internal areas with direct natural light. In such circumstances there are various ways of "borrowing" light from other rooms that are better lit—in effect, of making the available light in a space go further.

Internal windows, either open or glazed, will help to spill light through from sunny rooms to darker, more enclosed spaces. Substituting glass for solid panels in doors has a similar effect: fanlights or transoms over entranceways are obvious examples. Solid partitions, enclosing stairwells or internal rooms that lack windows, can be built of translucent materials such as glass brick, which lets in light but obscures views. And at the simplest level, the strategic placement of a large mirror, to reflect a window, multiplies the effect of light dramatically.

Right: A Japanese-style partition blocks only a small degree of light but provides a greater degree of privacy. The blurred outlines seen through the screen have a mysterious quality.

Left: Semitransparent fabric screens out unwelcome views without blocking the light. The material is thin enough to reveal the decorative pattern of glazing bars on the arched windows.

Right: Gauze, lace, voile, and other fine, translucent fabrics make perfect lightweight window treatments that diffuse bright sunlight but will not obscure natural light.

Colored and etched glass also have their place. The delicate filigree of light and shade that is cast when daylight is screened by panels of lace; the moody, geometric, slanted bands of light and dark thrown on walls and floor by half-open venetian blinds; or the pools of soft color caused by light shining through colored glass all create magical light effects.

All of these strategies are designed to maximize natural light or to moderate its effects in ways that add vitality to the interior. But in warmer climates or areas of the world that experience long, hot summers, natural light is generally so strong that the

Above left and right: Translucent glass panels over venetian blinds diffuse and filter the light in intriguing ways, while a similar effect is achieved by using a semiopaque plastic laminate to cover window casements.

Right: Plain cotton shades are a contemporary classic, providing just enough light control in bedrooms and living areas without shrouding the room in complete darkness.

question of its control becomes more important. In such circumstances, the interior needs to provide a shady and restful refuge from dazzling glare and uncomfortable heat levels. Smaller windows set in deep jambs, verandas and porches that surround the house with a transitional temperate zone, and slatted shutters, awnings, and blinds that screen the windows are all traditional ways of cooling the interior and taking some of the power and brilliance out of direct sunlight.

Above: Venetian blinds offer optimum light control, ranging from near complete transparency to total screening. Left partially open, they create patterns of light and shade.

Above right: Slatted blinds come in a variety of different materials and colors. Aluminum blinds have a hard edge, while wooden slatted blinds create a warmer effect.

Right: A kitchen/dining area is flanked by an acid-etched glass screen. The glass is held from behind by a stainless-steel support so the panels appear to float. Each can pivot individually so light can be controlled to a fine degree.

Far right: A glass end wall is screened by six pivoting curved glass panels faced with a thin veneer of birch wood.

People have always lit their homes. Rushlights, candles, oil lamps, and gasoliers are but a few of the devices employed in previous centuries to provide some illumination during the hours of darkness. Today, however, artificial lighting almost exclusively means electrical light. In little over a century, we have become so accustomed to its brightness, convenience, and practicality that it is almost impossible to conceive of any interior space without it. But although we may take its many good qualities for granted, in some ways we have still not yet learned how to handle its effects to best advantage.

Principles of lighting

When the celebrated American inventor, Thomas Edison, patented his incandescent light bulb in 1879, the electric age had well and truly arrived. Edison was not the first to come up with the idea of electric light, nor was his bulb the first patented design, but he was solely responsible for making this inspirational and revolutionary invention a successful and practical product. It might almost be true to say that Edison created a demand for electricity itself, by creating an electrical product that everyone suddenly wanted. It is small wonder that the light bulb has since come to symbolize the quintessential "bright idea."

With the arrival of electricity, domestic life soon became much more comfortable and convenient. The light bulb rapidly supplanted other forms of artificial lighting, and by the early decades of the twentieth century, electric lighting was already an established feature in many homes. Its numerous advantages over other forms of artificial lighting were readily apparent. Electric light was much safer than burning animal fat, wax, oil, or gas indoors; it was easier to operate and instantly responsive to

the flick of a switch; and, above all, it was clean. Over a century later it is difficult to appreciate just how dingy and dirty the old forms of artificial lighting (and heating) could be. Walls and ceilings, continually discolored by fumes from gas jets and smut from candles, had either to be decorated in such a way as to disguise the dirt or repainted and repapered with depressing regularity. Electric light brought about a new quality of light in more than one sense, since it made it more practical for interiors to be decorated in lighter, brighter colors. For the first time, there was a reasonable expectation they would stay that way.

Above: Pale furnishings and decoration make the most of natural light streaming in through the window. The curved floor lamp adds supplementary illumination for reading.

Left: A striking contemporary table lamp, with its graphic circular shade, throws light back onto the walls and upward, creating a good level of general illumination. The small table lamp provides focused bright lighting for the seating area.

In the early days of electrification, bulb wattages were low. By today's standards, the light emitted from such bulbs was fairly dim, weak enough for many early light bulbs to be left unshaded. The first house in New York City to be lit electrically was the palatial mansion of the millionaire financier J. Pierpont Morgan, in 1883. A contemporary illustration of the drawing room reveals the unintentionally amusing contrast of ornate "Pompeiian" decorations and rich furnishings lit by dozens of single bare light bulbs hung from the ceiling around the perimeter of the room.

Despite the relatively dim wattages of early electric lights, many people soon began to comment unfavorably on their uncomfortable dazzle and glare. Today, we expect to be able to see what we want to see when we want to see it. It is all too easy to forget that, in previous centuries, such revealing levels of

artificial illumination were rare. It is evident from scenes in many nineteenth-century novels, for example, that it was far from unusual to enter a candlelit drawing room after nightfall and be unable to make out the faces of all those who were gathered there. Electric light may have brought an end to such obscurity, but it introduced an almost painful brightness in its place. Critics remarked that it robbed fine rooms of "privacy and distinction," and attempts were made early to shade bulbs with colored silk or stained glass to soften the glare and tint the whiteness of the light. And it was not long before electric lights began to be hidden, fitted, for example, behind molding.

Technically lighting has improved immeasurably since the early days of electrification. But, in many situations, its effects are still no better orchestrated. Many homes today are overly bright but,

Far left: Table and floor lamps are mainstays of traditional or period styles of decoration, creating warm pools of light at strategic points in an interior.

Left: Symmetry is a useful ally when planning lighting. This pair of wall-mounted shaded lights can be swung across to provide light exactly where it is required at either end of a sofa.

Right: A glass lantern makes a handsome and welcoming focal point in a spacious entrance hall. Central lighting can sometimes be too dominating, but here the effect is softened by the addition of a pair of wicker-shaded table lamps sited in front of a mirror.

paradoxically, possess too few sources of light. The result is either a harsh and uncomfortable glare or a bright diffused level of illumination that cancels out any possibility of drama or interest—exactly the same basic disadvantages that were first remarked upon nearly a hundred years ago.

A radical reappraisal of lighting can provide one of the most dramatic, immediate, and economical ways of changing an interior space and our perceptions of it. Following on from observations on enhancing natural light, it is possible to draw out a few basic principles for good artificial lighting.

Many of these principles address the fundamental importance of avoiding glare. Glare is caused when there is too great a disparity between the brilliance of the light source and its surrounding

context. It is inherently uncomfortable because the eye is unable to accommodate such extremes readily, and therefore the process of continually adjusting between light and dark creates a feeling of tiredness and unease. Since the eye's natural tendency is to try to flatten or "correct" such discrepancies in the surrounding light levels, where lighting conditions give rise to glare there is always a great risk of eyestrain. Watching a bright, flickering television screen in the dark is bad for your eyes for precisely this reason. So is reading a book in a dim or darkened room, with only a task lamp at your side casting a bright flood of light onto the white page. Everyone is familiar with the unwelcome, almost painful, experience of being suddenly dazzled and blinded by the strong glaring beam of oncoming headlights. Perhaps less severe, but no less uncomfortable, are rooms that are lit by a single unshaded source.

Conceal sources

Lighting designers are fond of stating that when you walk into a room, you should see light, not lights. While this is not necessarily true in every single circumstance, it does sum up succinctly one of the basic principles of good lighting. A light source that is blindingly obvious is likely to be too bright and, therefore, to be causing unwelcome glare.

There is a wide variety of ways in which a light source can be concealed. First, the entire light, both the fixture and the bulb, can be hidden from view; second, the bulb can be shaded; or third, direct light from the bulb can be reflected by some means.

Concealed lights can take one of several different forms. The fluorescent strip hidden behind a baffle or mounted behind a cover strip under a row of kitchen wall cabinets is a concealed light; so is a floor-standing uplight placed behind a piece of furniture or a large leafy plant; so is more architectural lighting in the form of molding lights or lights recessed in display cabinets. Hiding the source in this way means that we see no direct light, just a gentle illuminating effect on surrounding surfaces.

Shading is an obvious way of concealing the light source. The ubiquitous Chinese paper shade, a cheap and cheerful solution in many households, transforms the piercing glare of a bare bulb into a glowing circle of diffused light. Lampshades, whether made from cotton, parchment, metal, or glass, perform the same function.

Reflecting light will also conceal a light source. At its simplest, this can entail the substitution of an ordinary bulb with one that has a silvered bowl. This is particularly effective for pendant lights where the shade is open at the base. The metallic cap over the end of the bulb reflects its light backward and bounces it off the shade. Many types of halogen light have reflectors built into their design to soften the direct effect of the source.

Above: Simple lighting ideas can create dramatic effects. Uplighters concealed within baseboard plinths accent the original and unusual plaster decoration framing the window.

Left: Fluorescent strip lighting concealed behind a baffle enhances the textural quality of an unpolished marble bathroom surface without dazzling the eye.

Right: Warm fluorescent strip lighting concealed within a vibrant blue-painted cavity transforms an existing chimney breast into a glowing focal point.

Light walls and ceilings

Lighting a room is a question of lighting a volume of space. The old arrangement of the central lighting fixture, either casting its light down or diffusing it in all directions, works against spatial quality by making the walls feel as though they are closing in. In contrast, bouncing light off an expanse of wall or ceiling generates a mood of expansiveness. Lighting walls and ceilings means using these surfaces as giant reflectors.

Wallwashers, angled spotlights, and wall-mounted uplights can all be used to create this effect. In most cases, the light source itself is concealed, and the diffusion is created by reflection or the spread of light on the surfaces. The result is a good general level of background light as well as a soft, restful atmosphere.

This page: A combination
of recessed low-voltage
downlights used as wall
washers and 300-watt
halogen uplights mounted
on the wall generates a
great sense of vitality.

Far left: Serge Mouille's
wall-mounted "Tripod" light
from the 1950s makes a
graphic statement in a
contemporary interior,
washing the walls with light.

Increase the number of light sources

Many homes that have a poor quality of light generally have too few lights. People are often unwilling to introduce more lights on the grounds that the room is already "bright enough" and more lights will only increase the level of illumination unnecessarily. However, increasing the number of light sources means that each individual light need not be so bright. Taken as a whole, the overall level of illumination need not increase.

A scheme where several lights do the job of one or two has obvious aesthetic advantages. If each light is of a relatively low level of brightness, the risk of glare is diminished because there will be less contrast between the light and its surroundings. On the other hand, one or two overly bright lights will inevitably cause uncomfortable extremes of light and dark in the interior.

There are also practical advantages. Increasing the number of light sources means that it is possible to specifically deliver light to chairside, bedside, desk, counter, or tabletop—the exact spot where it is needed. Single light sources may provide an adequate general level of illumination, but they will always lack the ability to be focused on a particular task or position.

Left and above: Open-plan areas need carefully judged lighting effects to avoid becoming either bland or intimidating. In this series of interconnecting spaces, there is the sense that light is coming from all directions. Downlights and pendants are combined with wall lights to highlight distinct areas of activity.

Create pools of light and shade

Related to the concept of increasing the number of light sources in an interior is the idea of arranging lights to create a series of overlapping pools of light and shade.

Light is indivisible from its partner, shadow. In fact, it is shadow, rather than light, that reveals the form and texture of objects. You can appreciate this more fully when you consider how the contour of a frontally spotlit object is flattened, whereas the same object, when lit from the side, will possess areas of shadow that reveal and define its basic form. In the same way, grazing a textured surface with a flood of light throws up its surface irregularities where shadows fall in the hollows.

Above: Light works hand in hand with architectural detail. A bright table lamp emphasizes the bold graphic impact of a flight of cantilevered stairs.

Right: Light is intrinsically inviting. An adjustable floor lamp provides illumination for reading or relaxing, balanced by a softer, diffusing light on the side table.

Creating pools of light and shade in an interior adds atmosphere, vitality, and a certain sensual quality. We are naturally drawn to light as we are drawn to sunny spots, and by arranging lighting so there are different focal points in a room, we create an inherent progression or movement through the space as well as setting up cozy circles or enclosures that will draw people together.

At the same time, where shadows fall between the light sources, there is the opportunity to reveal form and texture. A diffused overhead light source creates a bland atmosphere precisely because the light is flat and even. Lighting that makes interesting patterns of shade introduces a lively and tactile quality to surfaces and materials.

Above: Sidelighting an object reveals its contours and throws intriguing and decorative shadows onto a bare wall.

Build in flexibility

Lights that can be moved, adjusted, angled, or dimmed provide greater creative scope than immovable arrangements. Lighting depends on an infrastructure of electrical servicing, which has its own inherent limitations. By making sure the effect of individual lights can be altered, a lighting plan can remain responsive to changing circumstances and needs.

Lighting requirements can and do change on a daily basis. Dimmable lights are an obvious way of providing the means to alter atmosphere and mood. Lights that can be swiveled or angled to highlight various tasks and activities permit these activities to take place in different locations as the need arises.

Right: Cheap and versatile, clip-on loft lamps deliver accent or task light wherever it is required. They are easy to position, so are ideal for experimenting with different angles and effects.

Below: Tiny angled halogen downlights wash a wall and accent a painting. They are more flexible than stationary picture lighting and can be adjusted to suit changing displays.

Consider color and texture

Lighting, as mentioned previously, cannot be considered in isolation from decorative choices of color and texture. But different light sources also have an impact on the way existing colors and textures are perceived. Incandescent, the most common form of home lighting, has a warm, yellowish cast that makes it flattering to the complexion. Halogen, by contrast, emits a much cooler, whiter light that is "truer" to colors.

Texture can also be affected by the type of light source you choose. Frosted bulbs diffuse light more than clear varieties and hence cast softer, less defined shadows. Small bulbs, because the light source is less diffused, also create stronger, sharper shadows.

Opposite page: The warm glow of incandescent light is innately homey and hospitable, a perfect complement for soft furnishings and wooden finishes.

This page: Low-voltage halogen downlights combined with concealed fluorescent strip lighting create a crisp, contemporary look accentuating the sculptural planes of walls and spatial dividers.

Decorate with light

Our eyes are delighted and entranced by light and light effects. Every lighting scheme should have room for some elements of purely decorative lighting—that is, lighting that serves little or no practical purpose in terms of overall or task illumination, but simply serves to intrigue and enchant.

Left: Tom Dixon's "Jack" light—part light, part seat—makes a witty addition to a contemporary interior. Made of molded plastic, the design is available in a choice of colors.

Above, left and right: Unusual lamps contribute decorative flair. Organic shapes, such as the "marble dust" stone lamp, complement clean modern lines. More overtly sculptural is the "reverse" lamp shape cut out of bronze.

Into this category fall many types of light that emit low levels of illumination, enough merely to light up themselves, but are intrinsically pleasing to the eye. Christmas tree lights are an obvious example; other varieties include colorful, sparkling, or sculptural lamps that bring the art of lighting alive. We do not "need" such lights to see by, but their magical quality adds an element of surprise to the interior that enhances our enjoyment of space. Tiny lamps with shades made from glass beads add accents of jeweled color; organic forms transform light into sculpture.

Moving light, such as the flickering, dancing flames of fire or candles, is equally evocative. For all its variety and practicality, artificial electrical light has yet to capture this beguiling and seductive element of mobility. With their mesmeric quality and strong traditional associations, such "natural" light sources act as a potent link to the past, restoring that all-important dimension of intimacy and distinction.

Choosing light

The process of choosing lighting can be fraught with pitfalls. Lighting stores, showrooms, and in-store departments offer a beguiling and bemusing range for the uninitiated consumer. In such dazzling surroundings, it is easy to succumb to an impulse purchase, seduced just by the appearance of a light fixture. The choice of light sources complicates matters still further. Incandescent or halogen? Clear, frosted, or silvered-bowl bulbs? Which will deliver the type of light you really require?

There is nothing fundamentally wrong with choosing a light fixture simply because you love the way it looks. But the light must also do its job properly—it must function effectively in the particular context in which you intend to use it. A light fixture is not merely a style statement. Superficially, the fixture may be traditional or contemporary, discreet or flamboyant, but its primary purpose is to control the direction and spread of light. Depending on its design, it may diffuse,

reflect, or concentrate the light emitted from the source, and the effects created will be very different.

The light source introduces its own set of parameters. First and foremost, it is important to remember that what you are buying is *light*, not *a* light.

To gain a practical understanding of lighting, it is not necessary to master the complex calculations of the professional lighting designer or to immerse yourself in the jargon of the trade. The average home interior does not need detailed measurements of lighting or lux levels to be lit effectively, while most retailers would be baffled by a request to see their selection of "luminaires." Nevertheless, a working familiarity with the various sources of light and the common categories of fixture is an important prerequisite for making an informed choice, and this chapter explores the enormous variety of light sources and fixtures that are currently available.

Before choosing a light fixture, it is essential to consider what *makes* the light—the light source itself. The light source is what emits light, its point of origin. The sun is a natural light source; flames from a fire or a candle are artificial sources that we like to consider natural. Today, most artificial home light sources are those familiar tungsten-filament lamps, in common parlance, light bulbs. Over the past decade or so, halogen has been added to the home lighting repertoire, while recent improvements to fluorescent lights have made this type of light source more attractive and suitable for the home.

Choosing a light source

Most home lighting is produced in two ways: by incandescence or fluorescence. Incandescence occurs when an electric current is passed through a filament, causing it to heat up and glow. Fluorescence occurs when an electrical charge passing through a gas-filled tube excites the gas to emit invisible radiation, which in turn reacts with a phosphor coating inside the tube to cause a glow. Types of incandescent lighting include tungsten (tungsten filament), tungsten halogen, and low-voltage tungsten halogen. Fluorescent lighting is available in standard, compact, and miniature formats. Fluorescent light sources also include other "discharge" lamps, such as metal halide, low- and high-pressure sodium, high-pressure mercury, and neon, but these tend as yet to have few household applications.

The more economical and energy-efficient light sources, such as fluorescent, tend to have longer lifespans. But lifespan can also be affected by the way the lamp is used. Frequently switching an incandescent bulb on and off shortens its life dramatically, for example, while some bulbs function better in certain positions.

Lifespan itself can be a relative measure. Incandescent bulbs function at full capacity until they burn out, while fluorescent bulbs do not fail suddenly but gradually fade away in a slow, continuous decline of light level. Using a dimmer switch can extend the lifespan of some bulbs considerably.

Both fluorescent and incandescent light sources are powered by electricity, but they make light in different ways, have different advantages and disadvantages, and affect color differently. For an explanation of how different light sources affect the quality of light and color, turn to pages 168–171.

Above: In addition to the familiar "bulb" shape, incandescent lamps are also produced in tube and strip formats. These bathroom lights consist of 500-millimeter tungsten tubes butted together to form a linear unit and fitted with a dimmer.

Left: Halogen downlights pick out a kitchen counter, which is underlit by blue fluorescent tubes so that it appears to float.

Incandescent light

The oldest and still the most common home light source is the tungsten-filament, or GLS (general lighting service), bulb. The basic design has altered very little since its invention over one hundred years ago: a coil or filament is encased within a thin glass bulb that contains either a vacuum or a mixture of inert gases. (The first incandescent bulb featured a carbon filament, but this was replaced in 1907 by tungsten, which has a higher melting point and generates more light.) Electricity is passed through the filament, which heats up rapidly until it glows white hot. With time, the metal in the filament evaporates, gradually blackening the bulb with deposits and weakening the filament to the point that it can no longer carry the current. At this point, the bulb "burns out."

Incandescent bulbs have many advantages, not least of which is their sheer familiarity. Widely available in a variety of everyday outlets from supermarkets to convenience stores, they have become a basic household provision. Years of association with this type of light source has accustomed us to its particular characteristics, so much so that we consider it "normal"

household light. Cheap, readily available, easy to use and replace, and warm in tone, it has much to recommend it. But it also has certain disadvantages that might not be readily apparent.

The overriding aesthetic characteristic of incandescent light is its warmth (see Light and color, pages 168–171). Technically, incandescent bulbs emit most of their light in the yellow to red end of the spectrum and have a color temperature of around 2,900 degrees Kelvin. This gives the light a warmish cast, only slightly cooler than the light from a candle. At the same time,

Above left: Incandescent lighting is particularly welcome at the bedside. These polished brass swing-arm wall-mounted lamps use three-way bulbs so light levels can be varied.

Above center: Directoire in inspiration, these wall sconces have mirror backs to multiply the effect of the light.

Above right: Incandescent downlights, recessed in the ceiling and top of a bookcase, provide rich accent and ambient light.

Right: A floor lamp in the form of an attenuated candlestick, a common reference point for traditional lighting design.

Above: A neat contemporary wall-mounted fixture directs light in a broad wash both above and below the drum shade. The shade is made of closely woven raffia.

Above right: The "Costanza" floor lamp by Paolo Rizzatto is a succinct modern update of the classic standing lamp. The stem is telescopic so the height can be easily adjusted.

incandescent light has no unacceptable "spikes" in its spectral pattern (see Light and color, page 168–171), which makes it good for color rendering. Inherently intimate, incandescent light is flattering, reassuring, and cozy. Such visual characteristics make incandescent light appealingly atmospheric, especially at lower wattages, and a good complement for warm styles of decoration.

There are many practical advantages, too, many of which center on ease of operation. Incandescent bulbs require no additional equipment—or control gear—but can be run directly from the main electricity supply. Unlike other types of bulb, which need to warm up before they reach full illumination, they provide instant light at the touch of a switch. They are readily dimmed. They contain no toxic chemicals, which means they pose no disposal problems. And they are cheap to replace and produce.

Right: The wide base of the shade on this table lamp spills a broad pool of light down onto the desk. The swivel arm means light can be directed wherever it is needed.

Above left and right: Incandescent is the most fitting light source for these two pairs of table lamps. Symmetrical arrangements are well suited to more traditional interiors.

Below: Kitchen lighting need not create a white and sparkling effect. Here, concealed incandescent downlights illuminate a kitchen counter in a flood of warm golden light.

Added to these practical advantages is a versatility of design that facilitates the creation of a host of different lighting effects. Incandescent bulbs are available in a wide choice of shapes, sizes, wattages, and types, from tiny candle bulbs to spotlights, PAR (parabolic aluminized reflector) lamps, silvered-bowl bulbs, and linear tubes. The bulbs themselves may be clear, frosted, or colored. Wattage ranges from 15 to 200 watts.

However, incandescent bulbs do have significant disadvantages. In terms of converting energy into light, they are the least efficient of all light sources, converting a huge proportion of the energy into heat (over 90 percent), which is why they are hot to handle. As a result, such bulbs cannot be used too close to flammable materials such as fabric, paper, wood, or plastic shades. Since most bulbs are thin, lamps cannot be used outdoors, as sudden temperature variations might cause the glass to crack. (The PAR lamp, constructed of strong pressed glass, is one exception.)

Incandescent has the shortest life of all light sources. Measured as RAL (Rated Average Life)—the number of hours that half of such bulbs last when left on continuously—their lifespan is a mere 1,000 hours. (Again, an exception is provided by PAR lamps, which last twice as long.) Their cheapness to buy is substantially

offset by their expense to run, so they are rarely used in large-scale commercial applications. More robust, longer-lasting incandescent bulbs are available, sold as "double life." Some specialized outlets advertise bulbs that are claimed to last sixteen times as long as a normal incandescent bulb. They have stronger filaments and special compounds of gases in the bulb to prevent blackening; the downside is a higher price and lower light output.

Halogen light

Tungsten halogen, or halogen as it is popularly known, is a relative newcomer to the home scene. As the name suggests, halogen is the additional component. Mixed with the gases in the bulb, halogen interacts with the evaporated tungsten in such a way that it is redeposited on the filament. This prolongs the life of the bulb and means that it does not become blackened when run at full voltage. The filament burns at higher temperatures than in the standard incandescent bulb and the process requires a higher gas pressure. Hence, bulbs are smaller and made of quartz to withstand the increased heat.

Because the filament burns at much higher temperatures, the light cast by a halogen lamp is markedly whiter or "cooler" than standard incandescent, with a color temperature of more than

Above: This halogen "candle" light delivers cool, crisp light in an elegantly minimal fitting.

Right: Low-voltage downlights are a modern lighting classic. The clean, clear tones are perfect for contemporary interiors.

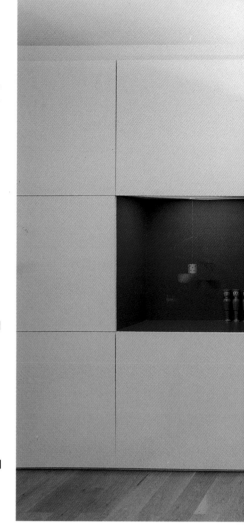

Far left and left: Halogen lighting is small and discreet, making it easy to conceal the source. As hidden uplighting on top of kitchen cabinets or downlighting integrated into ventilation hoods (far left) or in the form of minimal downlights (left), the effect is to focus attention on the quality of the light itself, rather than the fixture.

Right: Where the emphasis is on sculptural form and clean lines, halogen is a good choice. A 300-watt halogen uplight combined with low-voltage downlights used as wall washers serve to accent spatial volume.

Below left: Low-voltage halogen on a curving minimal track dots points of light around a living area.

3,000 degrees Kelvin and a wavelength pattern that is more evenly balanced across the color spectrum (see Light and color, pages 168–171). The result is an intense, sparkling white light that makes colors seem clearer and more sharply defined. Crisp, bright, and dramatic, it is not surprising that halogen found its original applications in theatrical and display lighting and in restaurants, where color fidelity is of prime importance.

In the home, standard household-current halogen which, like incandescent, can be run directly off the household current, scores highly wherever clear, bright light is needed. Of all the light sources suitable for household use, halogen is the closest to daylight, which makes it ideal in situations where concentrated work is carried out. Halogen uplights or downlights create white background light, which complements contemporary furnishings and architectural detail; spotlights add sparkle to displays.

Standard household-current halogen shares many of the practical advantages of incandescent. It can be dimmed, needs no control gear, and is instantly responsive to a switch. Bulbs are available in a variety of formats, including tubes, and in a range of wattages up to and above 700 watts. The bulbs can be used in conjunction with dichroic reflectors, whose mirrored backs help to disperse the increased heat generated. Lifespan is up to 3,000 hours.

The disadvantages are also similar. Standard household-current halogen is as energy-inefficient as incandescent and generates a considerable amount of heat, which can restrict its applications in the home. Heatproof fixtures are essential. Expensive to run, bulbs are also more expensive to buy and less readily available.

Since the bulb wattages are generally lower, they are more energy-efficient, making them cheaper to operate. At these lower voltages, the bulbs emit as much light as ordinary incandescent bulbs of the same rating. The low voltage also means that the lamps can be safely suspended from unsheathed wires, with such "bare wire" installations creating dramatically minimal effects in large open spaces. However, because the lights are so small, there is a temptation to use more of them. This strategy is a mistake, both practically and visually. Large numbers of low-voltage lights will raise the heat level considerably and will create an atmosphere that is definitely more retail than domestic. If they overheat they may also become a fire hazard.

The principal disadvantage of low-voltage lighting is that a transformer is required. Originally, transformers were bulky, required ventilation, and generated much heat. Concealment within ceiling spaces posed a fire risk and led to problems of access when maintenance was required. Now, however, small, lightweight electronic transformers have been introduced that can be integrated to form a fairly unobtrusive part of the fixture itself, or neatly incorporated behind a downlight, for example. Low-voltage halogen bulbs have a lifespan of about 3,000—3,500 hours and come in a range of wattages from 15 to 50 watts.

Below: Small pendant fixtures housing halogen bulbs make a practical and unobtrusive choice for kitchen lighting.

Low-voltage halogen

The recent introduction of halogen bulbs that can be run at lower voltages has increased the popularity of this type of light source. Low-voltage halogen systems, a rarity a decade ago, are now commonplace in many contemporary interiors.

Low-voltage halogen has the same basic aesthetic characteristics as the standard household-current version: it provides a crisp, white light that is good for color rendering and is dimmable. But the bulbs are much smaller and more compact, giving the light source a sparkling effect and making it much more discreet. It is small wonder that these tiny twinkly lights found their original application in window display and retail environments.

In the home, the applications are similar. Low-voltage halogen scores highly for unobtrusive accent and display lighting. The miniature size of the bulbs mean that reflectors can be more precise, allowing the light to be concentrated into a narrow beam, highlighting whatever you want to bring into focus, from a countertop to a decorative collection. Integral dichroic reflectors, which direct light forward and heat through the back of the bulb, are typical, although there are also separate capsule bulbs.

Fluorescent light

Until the last decade or so, fluorescent was the light everyone loved to loathe. With good reason: fluorescent light may be economical, energy-efficient, and long-lasting, but it is typically flickery, harsh, and sickly in appearance. While nominally "cool," with a color temperature closely approximating natural daylight, it has peaks in the green and orange parts of the spectrum and accordingly distorts colors and casts an unhealthy-looking pallor on complexions and interior decoration alike. Such detrimental visual characteristics have rightly seen the fluorescent tube largely relegated to more utilitarian areas of the home— workshops, garages, and basements—where its practical

Left: Fluorescent, once reviled by interior decorators and lighting designers, has recently been rediscovered by those in the stylistic vanguard. This kitchen is lit by fluorescents concealed behind a diffusing baffle of frosted glass.

Above: Narrow fluorescent tubes of various lengths have been fitted together to form a continuous concealed strip light.

advantages outweigh its stylistic drawbacks. Elsewhere, fluorescent—or strip lighting in its most familiar format— has had a tendency to appear brutal and unsympathetic.

But that was then. Fluorescent bulbs, more than any other light source, have seen continual improvements in design over the years, a process that has accelerated with the recent concern to produce more energy-efficient lighting for the home. By no means have all of the disadvantages been addressed, but new fluorescents have been devised that are somewhat warmer in appearance than their predecessors and hence more hospitable.

Fluorescence works in a different way from the other common home light sources. As briefly outlined before, an electrical charge passing through a tube filled with argon or krypton gas "excites"

the gas to produce invisible radiation, which in turn interacts with phosphors coating the inside of the tube, causing them to fluoresce, or glow. Since this process takes place at a low temperature, less energy is consumed. First devised in the late 1930s, fluorescent light quickly became a serious rival to tungsten in commercial and industrial buildings, where its extremely long life (up to 8,000 hours) and low operating cost constituted a powerful economic argument in its favor. Fluorescent bulbs do not fail suddenly, but gradually weaken over time.

Visually, fluorescent light is cool, bright, and diffuse, qualities that may be acceptable in workshops and showrooms but are less welcome in the home, where the light can seem both bland and chilly. Manufacturers have gone to some lengths to devise new types of fluorescence that are warmer in appearance—the color being determined by the precise mixture of phosphors in the coating. While some of these products represent a significant improvement over the standard fluorescent, the light still contains "spikes" in its spectral pattern (see Light and color, page 171), which makes it generally poor at color rendering. Unlike earlier versions, fluorescent lamps can now be dimmed, but the process is expensive. Other disadvantages have included the fact that there can be a considerable delay between switching and the

Far left: Microslim fluorescent tubes housed within birch-faced pivoting screens provide an even and controllable spread of light.

Center left: Custom bathroom light fixtures conceal microslim fluorescent tubes.

Left: Fluorescent strips concealed below storage units pick out a green recess behind the head of the bed.

Right and far right: Strip lighting can be used alone or with a diffusing panel to cast light over a wider area.

Far left below: At night, the fluorescent light in an indoor walkway transforms sandblasted glass into a glowing screen of light.

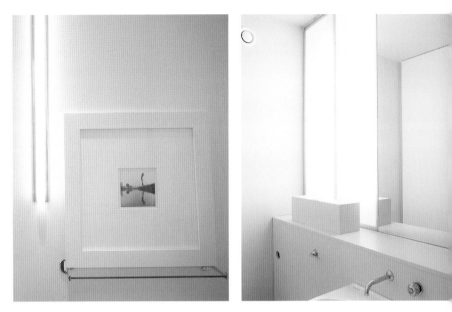

light coming on—the strike-up time—and the tendency of the lamps to hum and flicker. New designs are now available that address these problems, but they are much more expensive. The chemicals used in fluorescent lamps are highly toxic, and they must be disposed of carefully following manufacturers' instructions.

More radical developments have occurred in the field of compact and minifluorescents, which range from designs in which the tube is folded to make a compact shape to tiny tubes with a diameter no thicker than a pencil. There is also a new form of compact fluorescent in which the tube comes enclosed in a traditional frosted bulb. This design diffuses the light in the same way as an ordinary bulb and has a reassuring familiarity for those who find the tube a little alien in appearance.

As many of these fluorescent bulbs are now available with standard caps or adaptors, they can be used in nonspecialized fixtures, and are especially practical where hotter light sources would be dangerous or unsuitable, such as close to flammable materials. Their low energy consumption has greatly increased their popularity: using only 9 watts they can produce the same amount of light as a 40-watt incandescent bulb. Their operating cost is only a tenth of the cost of incandescent sources.

The process of development continues. As energy consumption becomes an increasing issue in the home, and manufacturers strive to improve the aesthetic characteristics of fluorescent lighting, these efficient and long-lasting bulbs are likely to become more common, not to mention desirable.

Left: Extremely fine fluorescent tubes provide an unusual lighting framework in an airy, spacious hallway.

Other sources

There are a number of other sources of artificial light, most of which fall into the category of discharge lamps. They include metal halide, low- and high-pressure sodium, and high-pressure mercury lamps. None, as yet, have household applications, although they are in widespread commercial, public, and industrial use. The lamps operate in a similar fashion to fluorescent bulbs, but use different types of gas or metal vapor. Generally very long-lasting and highly energy-efficient, they are essentially utilitarian rather than atmospheric. Some, as in the case of low-pressure sodium, are exceptionally poor at rendering colors accurately, making them suitable only for information lighting such as streetlights. Others have excellent color-rendering characteristics. Metal halide, which produces a cool

at a considerable distance from the actual light that is emitted, which in turn means that fiber optic lighting is exceptionally cool at the point of delivery. In another type of fiber-optic lighting, the coating is omitted from the strands, which then emit light all the way along their length.

The practical applications are considerable. The strands themselves can be touched, bent, or used underwater. Fiber optics makes good display lighting in museums—its very low UV content is ideal for illuminating paintings or textiles without damaging their fabric—or wherever materials need to be conserved and protected from heat, and in conditions that might otherwise be dangerous, such as swimming pools. Side-emitting fibers can be used, like neon, to outline architectural shapes. Fiber optics also provides an efficient way of lighting a large expanse decoratively, since a single bulb can control many small starry points of light.

white light close to daylight, is particularly good for backyard lighting and for lighting atria, since it accentuates greens and stimulates plant growth. Bulbs are generally large and robust, have a slow strike-up time, from seconds to minutes, require bulky control gear, and contain highly toxic chemicals.

Neon, otherwise known as cold cathode, produces a low level of colorful decorative lighting, familiar in commercial signs and public arts installations. Expensive and requiring specialized installation because of the high voltage at which it operates, neon has limited domestic potential, but can be used for striking architectural effects, behind coving or moldings, for example.

Fiber optics is a new form of lighting whose potential has not yet been fully explored. In fiber optics, light is shone down thin strands of coated fiberglass or acrylic. Due to internal reflection, no light escapes along the length of the strands but emerges at the ends. This means that the light source or bulb can be placed

More whimsically, it has been used for dramatic, magical effects: one luxury London hotel features fiber-optically lit faucets in the bathrooms, illuminating the running water. For the average person, familiarity with fiber optics is likely to be limited to those rather kitsch novelty table lamps popular a couple of decades ago, their moving upright strands like bristles tipped with light. Until technology develops further, however, fiber optics remains prohibitively expensive for more extensive use in the home.

Above: Until recently, the use of fiber optics in the home has been confined to the type of novelty effect displayed in this 1960s-style lamp with its vivid color changes.

Right: the magical potential of fiber optics is vividly illustrated by this unusual and imaginative bathroom arrangement. The large shower head includes a pressure switch that is linked to an integrated fiber optic light that illuminates every single droplet in a celebration of running water.

Terminology can be confusing. Technically, when lighting designers speak of the "lamp," they are referring only to the light source, or what is commonly known as the "light bulb." The "bulb" is simply the glass envelope that encloses the filament. Different light sources have strong associations with particular types of lamp. Tungsten-filament, for example, is most familiar in the traditional format; low-voltage halogen as tiny capsules in dichroic reflectors; fluorescent as tubes. Yet even within the same family of light source, there are many differences in size, shape, and design of bulbs.

Choosing bulbs

Obviously, when choosing a bulb, it is essential that it is correctly paired with its fixture. The bulb must have the appropriate design and size of cap to enable it to be plugged in, and it must be of no greater wattage than the fixture is designed to accommodate; otherwise, there will be a risk of overheating and even fire. Yet there are other variables that have more to do with the quality of light, and making a simple substitution of one type of bulb for another can have a significant impact on a lighting plan.

There are two basic types of bulb: those that emit light all around and those that project a beam of a certain width. The latter type is often known as a spotlight, but its correct technical term is a reflector bulb. A "spot" is in a reflector that emits a beam of light that is less than 30 degrees wide; a "flood" is a reflector that emits a beam greater than 30 degrees. Reflector bulbs are specially shaped and silvered inside to throw the light forward; they are generally used in conjunction with shaped or cowled fixtures that further control the spread of light. Bulbs that emit light all around tend to work best in fixtures that diffuse the light but conceal the source, such as shaded table bulbs or pendants; but they can also provide more directional light when used in uplights and downlights, for example.

With an incandescent bulb, the glass bulb surrounding the filament has a critical effect on the quality of the light that is shed. Bulbs may be clear, frosted, or colored, and come in different sizes and shapes. Fully transparent bulbs have the effect of making the light source seem smaller. Consequently, shadows are stronger and more crisply defined. For this reason, the light level will appear to be lower than that emitted from a frosted bulb of equal wattage.

Above: Tiny halogen capsules are designed to be used with dichroic reflectors, which diffuse the heat generated by the light source and help to focus the beam.

Left: The silvered-bowl bulb has a reflective metallic coating over the crown of the lamp, which reflects light backward and prevents uncomfortable glare.

Clear bulbs create atmospheric effects when employed in decorative pierced or punched fixtures such as lanterns, since they add definition to the pattern of shadows cast by the design.

Frosted bulbs diffuse the light and reduce glare. They create a soft, omnidirectional glow, which is comfortable and easy on the eye. Bulbs of greater opacity, such as opalescent bulbs, reduce glare still further. Globe and candle bulbs, which are intended to remain visible, are sometimes available with this type of bulb.

Colored bulbs range from the lurid to the subtle. Intensely colored bulbs may be amusing for creating theatrical effects at parties, but have little role in interior decoration. Pastel and soft-tone bulbs have been heavily marketed by manufacturers. They emit a soft light that is gently tinted in a particular shade. More specialized in application are daylight-simulation bulbs, which have blue bulbs. These produce a whiter light than standard incandescent and offer truer color rendering, both of which attributes are valuable for artists, designers, and other craftspeople who need to able to judge color relationships accurately.

Incandescent bulbs come in a variety of shapes as well as the traditional form. Round globe bulbs, large and small, are commonly used to frame a makeup mirror or dresser. Candle bulbs, as the name suggests, are intended for use in sconces and chandeliers. Some candle bulbs are literally flame-shaped; others are designed to flicker and are merely decorative.

Low-voltage halogen bulbs can be bought in the form of tiny bulbs, called capsules, which throw light in every direction, or mounted in a dichroic reflector, which throws light forward while the heat generated by the bulb is reflected backward through the glass. The quartz envelope of halogen capsules must not be handled, as grease from the skin will become indelibly "fired" onto the surface of the glass when the bulb reaches its operating temperature. Such bulbs must be handled through a cloth or when wearing cotton gloves. If a bulb is inadvertently handled, it must be cleaned with alcohol before use. A representative selection of the wide variety of bulbs available today is shown on pages 176–177.

The cap is what allows the bulb to be plugged into the light fixture. There are a number of different designs. In the United States, the Edison screw (ES) is most common. The most popular cap in Britain is the bayonet (BC), whose twin prongs lock the bulb in place. Small versions of each type of cap are available. Standard household-current halogen bulbs are also available with either bayonet or screw caps. Low-voltage halogen bulbs generally come with either double pin caps or caps that twist and lock (TAL). New compact fluorescent bulbs are increasingly available

with screw or bayonet caps, allowing them to be plugged into a greater variety of light fixtures. Formerly, fluorescent bulbs exclusively required their own type of fixture.

There is a huge choice of other bulbs on the market for all types of fixtures and applications, from tiny lights to fit appliances to tubes that are designed to be mounted behind baffles for illuminating kitchen counters. Some of the more versatile of the specialized bulbs include silvered-bowl bulbs and PAR bulbs.

Invented in the late 1960s, silvered-bowl bulbs are standard incandescent bulbs with a reflective coating over the crown. This reflects the light backward when the bulb is used in a pendant position, or down when it is fitted upright. Originally designed to be used in conjunction with a parabolic reflector (a shaped fixture that produces a tight beam of light), silvered-bowl bulbs actually have much wider applications. In a table lamp, a bulb with a silvered bowl directs all the light down, allowing none to escape from the top of the shade. This produces a bright pool of light at the base of the lamp, an effect that both generates atmosphere and provides good local task lighting. In a pendant shade, the bulb reflects light backward off the shade to produce a more diffused effect with less glare. Silvered-bowl bulbs are more expensive than standard varieties, but last no longer. The silvered part is sometimes available as a separate cap that can be fitted over the crown of the bulb, making replacement more economical. There is also a small version of the bulb.

PAR bulbs (parabolic aluminized reflectors) have silvered backs that throw light forward in a strong beam. Available as either tungsten filament or tungsten halogen, they have a tough cast-glass casing with a lense front, allowing them to withstand sudden changes in temperature. In the United States, PAR bulbs are a popular feature of interior lighting schemes, but in Britain they are more commonly used for outdoor and security lighting. PAR bulbs have twice the lifespan of ordinary incandescent bulbs and come in a range of wattages and sizes.

Many contemporary designers do not share the conventional view that light bulbs are merely practical necessities that must be hidden from sight. The bare bulb is increasingly seen as an object of beauty by the lighting avant-garde. Designers such as Ingo Maurer have come up with witty variations on Edison's landmark invention—bulbs encased in bulbs and bulbs with wings (shown on pages 102–103). At the cutting edge, the wheel has turned full circle, with the bare bulb displayed for its own sake just as it was in the early days of electrification.

Left: From silvered-bowl to compact fluorescent, the wide variety of bulbs available is illustrated on pages 176–177.

From Philippe Starck's Miss Sissi lamp in colorful molded plastic to an antique Venetian cut-glass chandelier, from minimal downlights recessed in the ceiling to the ubiquitous paper shade, light fixtures display an incredible variety of style and function. Every year many lights that were originally designed for commercial or industrial use make the crossover to the home market, extending the choice still further. Technological advances have also broadened the scope. The whole field of lighting is currently experiencing an exciting period of great change, innovation, and development.

Choosing fixtures

The increased fluidity between commercial and home lighting design has been a lasting legacy of high-tech, while the classic products of progressive Italian manufacturers such as Arteluce, Flos, and Artemide have achieved permanent design status. Lighting has also had a particular fascination for many modern architects, and innovative postwar designs by famous names such as Eero Saarinen and Alvar Aalto remain in production.

In this age of miniaturization, minimal is a definite trend. Tiny low-voltage lights seamlessly integrated into walls, ceilings, and floors reduce lighting to its bare essentials. At the same time, lighting and light fixture design has become much more expressive. An organic use of materials and a playful, sculptural sense of form are displayed in the work of many contemporary designers. Lighting, suddenly, has become much more fun.

It is not surprising, given this immense variety, that light fixtures resist hard-and-fast categorization, but concentrating on function is an important first step in achieving a good quality of light. The prime function of a light fixture is to direct and control the spread or distribution of light. Some fixtures emit light all around, or omnidirectionally; others, such as table lamps, semidirectionally; the rest are purely directional: spotlights, floodlights, and wall washers fall into this category. Within such broad groupings further distinctions can be made, sometimes to do with the way a light functions and sometimes to do with how it is designed to be installed, mounted, or used. Inevitably, there are areas of overlap.

In the lighting trade, a light fixture is known as a luminaire and is defined as the fixture that holds the light source, or bulb, in place.

Above: A gleaming metal-and-glass uplight with a hard-edged aesthetic. The shape of the fixture provides a graphic demonstration of the way light will be directed.

Left: The playful, sculptural form of this contemporary floor lamp, with its obvious reference to the shape of kites, is typical of many of the exciting new designs available today.

Uplights

Uplights, or uplighters as they are also known, do just what their names suggest—they direct light upward. By using the ceiling as a giant reflector, they create a soft, diffused ambient light. The ceiling glows as if it were backlit, while the light levels fall away closer to the floor. The result is a good quality of background light, with more distinction and refinement than ambient light from a central source, and fewer shadows.

As sources of background light, uplights work best in rooms with fairly high ceilings. Architectural detail is a plus. If the uplight is too close to the ceiling, the area of reflectance will be too

Above left: Uplighting creates an expansive effect by directing light at the ceiling from where it is reflected to provide a good level of background illumination.

Above center: Uplighting can be a good way of enhancing the texture of wall surfaces and ceilings as well as highlighting attractive architectural detail.

concentrated and the light less soft and diffused: the greater the distance between the light and ceiling, the greater the area that will be lit. Similarly, uplights are wasted in rooms where the ceiling is painted a dark color: white or light-toned surfaces make the most of the effect. Fine cornices, moldings, coved or curved ceilings add to the general air of distinction.

Because the light is indirect and glare-free, uplights are ideal for studies and home offices where computer screens are in use. In these situations uplights work especially well in conjuction with halogen sources, which generate a brighter, whiter light.

Uplights can also be used as accents. Low-level cylindrical uplights, concealed behind a piece of furniture, collection of objects, or a large plant, cast theatrical light into corners, create evocative patterns of shadow, and enhance texture and relief.

There are many types of uplight on the market—and many other lights that lend themselves to creating an improvised uplit effect. The classic floor-standing uplight dates back to the early decades of this century, when it was a dramatic feature of many grand Art Deco interiors, such as hotel and movie theater foyers. While some designs retain this retro flavor, there are also numerous contemporary versions that are extremely elegant in appearance. As attention is largely directed at the effect of the light, the fixtures themselves tend to be very discreet, formal and plain, with slender metal uprights supporting shallow sandblasted glass or ceramic bowls: a good example is the Jill uplight from Arteluce (shown on page 72). Such fixtures, which produce a wide distribution of light, often look good in pairs, in symmetrical arrangements at the corners of rooms. More flamboyant are designs such as Montjuic (shown on page 72) by the renowned Spanish architect, engineer, and designer Santiago Calatrava,

Above right: Portable, versatile, and utterly contemporary, this sleek metallic floor-standing uplight is a sympathetic choice for a modern interior.

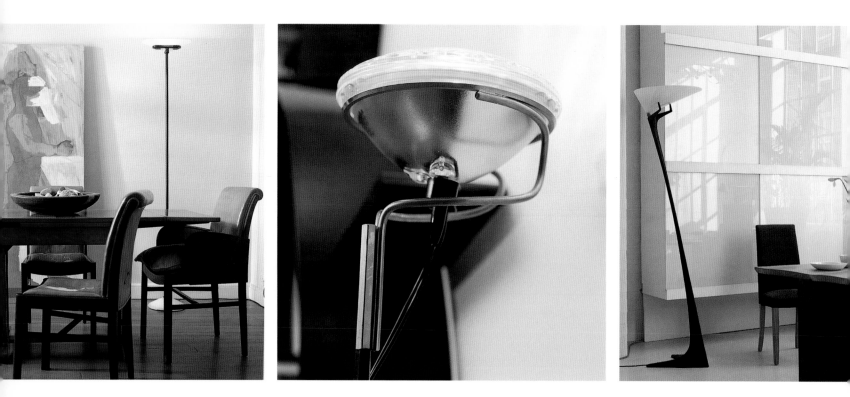

which reveals that designer's interest in skeletal, organic forms. Freestanding uplights tend to be both portable and flexible, allowing light to be delivered wherever it is needed, or to be easily adapted to changes in furniture layout.

Uplights also come in the form of wall-mounted fixtures. Again, discretion of design is typical. Shallow frosted glass or opaque ceramic dishes make unobtrusive fixtures; many can even be decorated in the same way as the wall finish to blend in completely. Some wall-mounted uplights are designed to spill a little light around the edge of the fixture to highlight their shape. This also has the effect of preventing the fixture from making too dark a contrast to the light it emits. More exuberantly, uplights with a period flavor are also available—in the form of Gothic capitals, classical brackets, or similar architectural flourishes. Wall-mounted uplights make excellent solutions for lighting halls and staircases.

On a more basic level, you can improvise an uplight in any number of ways. The simplest is to angle a spot or task light so that it directs all of its light at the ceiling; clip-on spots are

versatile in this respect. The spread of light will not be as wide, but this is nevertheless a good way of highlighting a dark corner of a room. Similarly, a small footlight can be placed on the floor behind a group of objects or plants, or on the top of a cupboard or shelves to create instant ceiling uplift. A fluorescent strip light concealed behind a molding or coving provides a safe, dramatic architectural accent. And any opaque shade suspended below a ceiling light—from a giant waxed umbrella to a reflective metal dish—will reflect the light up to bounce off the ceiling.

Like many other forms of light, uplights should be used in combination with other light sources. Without low-level bulbs and accent lights to create other focal points of interest, a room that relied solely on uplights could be bland and somewhat oppressive. Dimming the light level to take account of different moods during the day is also a good idea. The essence of uplighting is concealment of the source, which means that they should generally stand or be set at eye level or higher, unless the entire light is hidden from view. This also rules out their use in split-level spaces—looking down from a mezzanine into the glare of an uplight would be harsh and uncomfortable in the extreme.

Above left: The "Jill" uplight, designed for the Italian lighting design company Arteluce by King, Miranda, Arnaldi in 1978, is a contemporary classic.

Above center: Inspired by a car headlight, the "Toio" was designed by Achille and Pier Giacomo Castiglioni in 1965.

Above right: Santiago Calatrava's "Montjuic" uplight has an organic quality that reflects the designer's interest in natural forms. The light is diffused by the frosted glass bowl.

Right: Discreet placement of a floor-level uplight throws a splash of light upward from one corner of a room.

Downlights

Downlights, or downlighters, include a choice of fixtures designed to direct light down from a source high up in the room. Minimal in design but with maximum effectiveness, these lights have long proved indispensable in commercial and retail spaces as a means of providing concentrated light for work and display areas. In the home, downlighting has become much more common in recent years, particularly in kitchens, bathrooms, and halls—wherever unobtrusive but efficient light is required.

Downlights may be recessed or partially recessed in the ceiling or surface-mounted; they may also be either fixed or directional. Other variables include accessories such as mounting rings, baffles, louvers, and slotted covers, designed to spill light back across the ceiling and reduce glare. The beam of light emitted varies from narrow to wide. Recessed lights project a narrower beam than those that are partially recessed or surface-mounted.

Fully recessed downlights require a minimum of 5 inches ceiling space above to take the fixture (to ensure adequate ventilation). In situations where there is insufficient ceiling space, partially

recessed or surface-mounted fixtures should be used instead. All downlights should have heatproof covers over the terminals to reduce the fire risk and, to make absolutely sure that the fixtures have adequate ventilation, they should be installed by a qualified electrician (see page 187).

A wide range of designs is available to take different light sources, from standard line fixtures to tiny, discreet, twinkling low-voltage halogen lights with dichroic reflectors. Some incorporate suspended glass rings to diffuse glare. Adjustable "eyeball" downlights can be swiveled to alter the direction of the beam.

Above left: Downlighting has a theatrical quality, focusing attention on the high points of decor and furnishing.

Above right: Rooms that incorporate fixed or built-in features, such as bathrooms or kitchens, can be downlit more successfully than areas such as living rooms or bedrooms where you may want to retain a degree of flexibility.

Left: Low-voltage downlights recessed in the ceiling are a common solution to the problem of providing efficient lighting in kitchens. Local downlighting is also provided for counters.

Above left: Low-voltage downlighting accentuates the spatial quality of a minimal sleeping area and the transparency of the huge expanse of window.

Far left and left: Downlighting has a certain momentous quality, which can lend drama to displays of decorative objects.

Above right: The ultimate in concealed lighting combines low-voltage downlights with a warm fluorescent strip in a ceiling recess.

Above far right: Downlights recessed in a hall ceiling enhance the reflective surface of the flooring.

The great virtue of downlighting is its discretion. These basic circles of light, flush with the plane of the ceiling, have next to no stylistic associations of their own, which makes them compatible with every type of decor, from contemporary to traditional. In period rooms, where track lighting would be too conspicuous, downlights are a good means of providing both general or ambient light and focused accents. (In some period rooms, however, ceiling space may not permit recessed fixtures; while in others, where the fabric is of great architectural merit, cutting into plasterwork may be unacceptable.) In modern interiors, the sheer simplicity of downlights is perfectly in keeping. Downlights are usually controlled from a single switch near the door; dimmer controls extend the effects you can create.

But downlighting is not a universal panacea. Because downlights entail a fixed arrangement, they work best in contexts where there are already built-in features that limit the scope for changing the way the room is used. It makes more sense over the long term, for example, to downlight a kitchen counter, a bathroom sink, or a hall—areas where flexibility is not an issue—than to downlight living areas where fixed lighting can restrict options. Wherever downlights are installed, thought must be given to the subsequent ease with which maintenance can be carried out.

There can also be problems with the quality of light. Glare is an issue. Dimming can lower the levels to produce a gentler effect, but may reduce the efficiency of the lighting for working areas. Downlights tend to overlight horizontal surfaces, such as tables and counters, at the expense of vertical ones, such as walls, and consequently the overall atmosphere can become rather portentous and gloomy, particularly if there are not any supplementary sources of light. Rows of downlights, or downlights arranged around the perimeter of the ceiling, can also have a somewhat commercial feel. One solution is to opt for adjustable "eyeball" or directional downlights, which introduce a greater sense of variety by grazing the surface of walls and accentuating texture. Positioning must be given careful consideration, especially over working areas, so that the surface itself is illuminated and you are not trying to work in your own shadow.

On more decorative terms, downlighting is an excellent way of accenting objects, plants, and collections. Picking out an object with a beam shone down from above is highly dramatic, while eyeballs can be swiveled to wash a painting or picture with light. Similar effects can be achieved in dining areas, with downlights reflecting off white linen or more closely focused on centerpieces to create an intimate and celebratory mood.

Spotlights are pure drama. In the theater, the function of spotlighting is to highlight action, to focus the audience's attention on a particular area, or to isolate an actor in a circle of light. In the home, spotlights can provide a variety of lighting effects, from accent to more ambient illumination.

Early spotlights were obvious and bulky. With the development of low-voltage systems, a spotlight today can be little more than a pinpoint of light. In between, there is a great variety from which to choose, from surface- or track-mounted fixtures for walls, ceilings, or floors, to spotlights on freestanding supports, and clip-on designs that can go just about anywhere.

Spotlights are available in a wide choice of finishes, colors, shapes, and designs. Most common, for home use, are inexpensive neutral plastic fixtures, but brightly colored as well as steel, aluminum, and brass versions are also available. Spotlights tend to have a functional appearance, which is not surprising since the form or shape of the fixture helps to control the focus and direction of the light. Some contemporary designs are more

Left: The spotlight provides the opportunity to control light with exceptional precision, particularly with the addition of filters, diffusers, and framing shutters.

Spotlights

The spotlight was one of the very first light fixtures to migrate from the professional world into the home. The mainstay of stage lighting, spotlights also have a respectable history of use in the retail world as a simple but effective means of lighting displays and store windows. They first began to make an appearance on the home front in the 1960s and have since become an established part of the lighting repertoire.

As previously explained, technically speaking, a spotlight is a reflector light that projects a beam of less than 30 degrees, while a floodlight is a reflector light that projects a beam that is wider than 30 degrees. In practice, most people tend to refer to any kind of lamp or fixture that projects a controlled directional beam as a spotlight. Confusingly, recessed ceiling downlights are also often called spotlights: there is a certain interchangeability and ambiguity of terms in this area.

Right: A simple spotlight, consisting of an incandescent reflector bulb in a movable plastic casing, provides angled yet general illumination in a living room.

is needed; this versatility is a major advantage. Some have integral handles or levers that enable repositioning to be carried out without having to make direct contact with a hot fixture.

Spotlights, as might be expected, provide unbeatable accent light. Low-voltage halogen spots—or minispots—are especially valuable in this respect, picking out focal points in a sparkling white light. But their applications are not limited to display. In large open spaces they can be used as general background lighting, creating overlapping ambient pools of light that are more interesting and atmospheric than a uniform level of illumination. Fixtures made of two or three spotlights mounted together can be a useful substitute for a central light. Spotlights make good task lights for kitchens, although they can become greasy and dusty over time. They are not advisable for bathrooms, where there is the risk of water being splashed on the bulbs.

Despite their flexibility, proper positioning of spotlights is important, particularly for surface-mounted versions where some disruption of wall finishes is inevitable. Especially in kitchens or other working areas, care must be taken to avoid glare—dazzling light can present a hazard if you are using sharp tools or working with heat. Light must be angled so it falls across the work surface to prevent backlighting and the risk of working in shadow.

Above and right: Clip-on spotlights are cheap and versatile. Light can be directed at a display or working area or upward to provide background illumination.

overtly stylish, with a futuristic appeal of their own; there are also more retro-looking designs, simple rounded shapes that are available in matte metal or stove-enameled finishes.

Bulb and fixture are designed to work together to give a precise, controlled beam of light. The parabolic reflector is an early spotlight design, the cowl-shaped fixture focusing and reflecting light thrown backward by a silvered-bowl bulb. Most spotlights today take incandescent reflector bulbs that are silvered on the inside. Low-voltage halogen spotlights have dichroic reflectors, with mirrored or faceted backs that throw light forward but disperse heat backward.

Additional light control can be provided by diffusers, filters, and "barn doors," or framing shutters. The framing projector is a spotlight that incorporates shutters which can be adjusted to shape the light in a precise way. These tend to be expensive. Barn doors (the term orginated in theatrical lighting) are also used to reduce glare and to shape and define the light emitted from floodlights. Most spotlights can be tilted or swiveled to angle light wherever it

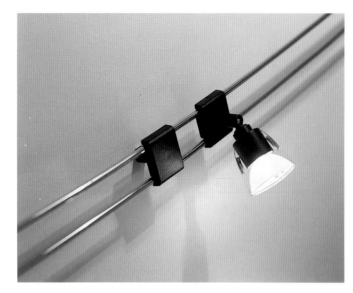

Track lighting

The development of track lighting, some thirty years ago, helped to boost the popularity of spotlighting in the home. Lighting tracks come in two basic forms. In its "free" form, the track acts as an extended power source, allowing a number of different lights to be connected along its length and moved about, providing an even greater degree of flexibility for positioning and angling light. The track, or "bus bar," carries the current, and lights are simply plugged in wherever they are required using a special connector. Safety devices ensure that the live track cannot be touched directly. A great advantage is that different light fixtures can be combined on the same track, provided they have the right connecting socket. In this way, a track can power spotlights in one part of the room and a pendant over a dining area in another. Many types of light fixtures and tracks from different manufacturers are now interchangeable.

In its "fixed" form, the track comes with between two and four light fixtures already attached to it. The individual lights cannot be repositioned along the track, but generally can be angled and swiveled. This is the most common type of track lighting on the home market, and most varieties are reasonably priced. Although

Above, left and right: Low-voltage track lighting is both refined and restrained. The brushed stainless steel track allows these picture lights to be accurately positioned.

Right and far right: Track lighting was once rather cumbersome and obvious. These low-voltage versions offer maximum flexibility with minimum visual intrusion.

Left: Track lighting offers the potential to combine pendant fixtures over tables and seating areas with spotlights to accent displays or provide more general illumination.

Below and right: So-called "bare wire" installations carry such low voltages that cabling can be left unsheathed, resulting in lighting arrangements with all the appeal of a trapeze act. The cables are tensioned between walls or between floor and ceiling, and individual lights can be positioned anywhere along their length. The larger the space, the better the effect.

Bottom: Shiu-Kay Kan's stylish and minimal Chopstick light is a particularly elegant example of a bare wire installation.

fixed track lighting lacks the versatility of free track, it offers a convenient package with a wide variety of applications.

Both free and fixed forms of track lighting are available in standard line and low-voltage versions. Free standard household-current track lighting is particularly popular in the United States. It comes with a remote transformer that is concealed in a ceiling space; fixed low-voltage track lighting normally has an integral transformer as part of the fixture. Power is delivered to one end of the track only.

Lighting tracks can be mounted vertically or horizontally, on the wall, ceiling, and even the floor. Straight sections are most common and can be connected to create longer runs or angled around corners. Curved track is also available, but is generally expensive. In high ceiling spaces, track can be suspended on

Above: Track lighting has a technical aesthetic and is best suited to modern interiors with strong contemporary details.

cables or rods to provide a means of uplighting or to make maintenance and access easier. Suspended track also allows the combination of uplights with spots, providing light in every direction.

Track lighting originated in the commercial sector and retains a slightly hard-edged image. Small runs of neutral-colored track or the more minimal low-voltage designs are less obtrusive for the home, but the essentially linear nature of track lighting makes it an eyesore in period rooms with fine architectural detailing.

The chief practical disadvantage is the risk of overloading. Free low-voltage systems are particularly vulnerable. The rating of the transformer dictates the number/wattage of the lights that can be installed; a second track and transformer are needed if more lights are required as the electrical capacity of the track is limited.

Bare-wire installations

A recent refinement of lighting track, barewire installations are the ultimate in minimalism. With a look-no-hands quality that is both appealingly basic and highly dramatic, a pair of tensioned cables supports tiny low-voltage lights that can be moved at will along the wiring. Since the cables carry a current of only 12 volts, they can be unsheathed and even touched with safety. They are tensioned from wall to wall or from ceiling to floor and connected via a transformer to a power source.

A variety of elegantly simple fixtures are designed for use with a bare-wire setup. SKK's Chopstick light (shown opposite), a tiny low-voltage light that rests across the cables on thin rigid arms, is a typically witty example. There are even mobile roboticized lights that can be remotely controlled to move along the wires.

Bare-wire installations are widely used for museum and display lighting, but are now becoming increasingly popular in contemporary interiors, especially in the large open spaces of converted lofts and warehouses, where their dramatic effect is displayed to greatest advantage.

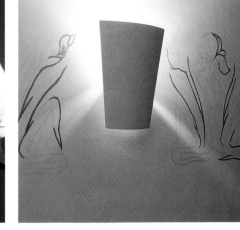

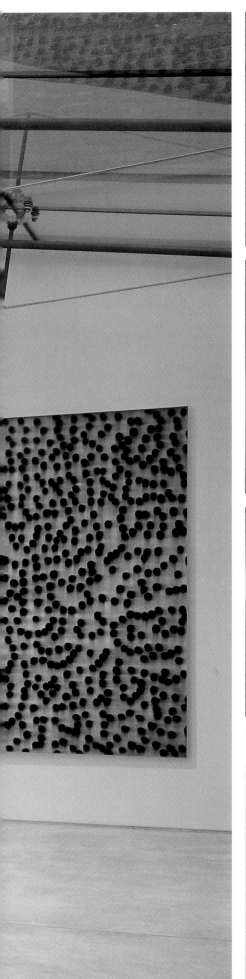

Wall lights

Like the ceiling, walls provide both a convenient and practical surface for mounting fixtures and a reflective plane to create a gentle source of ambient light. Wall lights can be directional, as in the case of wall-mounted uplights (see Uplights, pages 70–73), but more typically they emit light all around. Like lamps, wall lights come in a huge variety of designs, from period or traditional styles to the latest in contemporary fixtures.

Wall lighting provides a subtle form of background illumination that is calming, restful, and glare-free. Unlike central lights, which tend to focus a space around a point and generate a dull sense of uniformity, wall lights both allow greater fluidity of arrangement and have more inherent vitality. They often look best in pairs, flanking a sofa or headboard, for example; traditional designs in particular lend themselves to symmetry. Combined with a dimmer, wall lighting can provide flexible and responsive levels of ambient light in halls, living rooms, dining rooms, and bedrooms.

From torchères to candle sconces, girandoles to gasoliers, wall lighting has a long history, and one that is amply reflected in the design of traditional fixtures on the market. Many take the form of

Far left: Wall-mounted floodlights provide more focused illumination with the addition of barn-door attachments that can be adjusted to direct the spread of light.

Above and left: Wall lights come in a wide variety of designs, from the traditional to the cutting edge. The shape of the fixture will control the spread and direction of light. Shaded fixtures emit an all-around glow, while some designs throw light both up and down.

sconces, or supports for candles, with bracketed arms or branches that project from the wall. Reproduction electric candles are standard in many of these fixtures; some are astonishingly realistic—or amazingly kitsch, depending on your point of view. Some electric candles even pulse and flicker; others simulate melting wax. Similar to sconces are girandoles, or sconces with mirrored backs, a design originally intended to multiply the effect of candlelight. Candle bulbs can either be left exposed, in which case you should opt for low wattages to avoid glare, or shaded with small individual fabric or parchment shades.

Other styles with a period flavor include reproductions of turn-of-the-century gas or oil lamps. These typically are shaded with funnels or globes of glass, either colored, opaque, or etched, supported on sinuous curving metal arms.

Contemporary designs display an equal variety. In addition to wall-mounted uplights, there are fixtures that emit light omnidirectionally, often incorporating special features to reduce direct glare. A host of materials, including metal, plain ceramic, frosted glass, molded plywood, and fabric, have been employed by contemporary lighting designers to make organic, sculptural forms with great visual impact. Simple shapes look good in pairs, or in succession down the length of a wall; more asymmetric forms can be used successfully on their own as a focus of interest.

Wall washers

A specific form of wall lighting, wall washers are essentially downlights that bathe the wall in an even level of illumination. Usually mounted on the ceiling, either on track, recessed, or on the surface, they incorporate baffles or reflectors to direct light at the wall. Adjustable "eyeball" downlights, which can be readily positioned, are often used as wall washers.

Like uplighting, the effect is to create a soft, diffused background light by bouncing light off the surface of the wall, using it, in effect, as a reflector. The resulting sense of spaciousness and expansion and the discretion of the light source makes this type of lighting particularly sympathetic in sleek, contemporary interiors.

The quality of the wall surface is a key consideration. As with uplighting, wall washing is most effective where the wall is light-toned and smooth, to maximize reflectiveness. But textured surfaces can also be interestingly lit in this way, with the light accentuating the variations in the wall. Wall washers require careful positioning to avoid glare. The angle of the light must be such that those sitting close to the wall are not dazzled.

Left: An adjustable wall-mounted lamp can be repositioned according to requirements.

Above left: Halogen wall lights provide sparkling illumination.

Above center: An industrial-style fixture, with metal conduits carrying the wiring over bare brickwork.

Above right: Eyeball downlights, which are mounted in the ceiling, are one of the most common form of wall washers. The fitting can be swiveled (hence the name "eyeball") to direct a wash of light over the wall or to frame a specific area.

Central and hanging lights

Central lights are the *bête noire* of many lighting designers, and have had a more or less consistently bad press over the years. It is not difficult to see why. Bright, overhead light cast from a single pendant is a killjoy of the first order. At the flick of a switch, a room is immediately divested of any subtlety and atmosphere, mystery and intimacy. Instead of evocative contrasts of light and shade, there is flat, even illumination. Instead of the eye being drawn to points of light around the room at different levels, there is the oppressive static focus of the center.

Yet for all its potential disadvantages, the fixed central light remains a familiar lighting pattern. In older houses, the central molding is a survivor of the days of gaslight and candlepower. Often, where there is elaborate surrounding plasterwork, it is not a detail one would wish to ever eradicate but nevertheless it can look curiously superfluous if there is no central light suspended from it. There are also plenty of new houses that feature the same arrangement. The answer, if central lights are to remain a feature, is to devise ways of incorporating them within a more flexible and atmospheric lighting scheme.

Not all central lights have been tarred with the same brush. The popularity of the chandelier, for example, has never waned; in recent years, many contemporary designers have turned their attention to the reworking of this classic. And there are, of course, many situations in which central lighting provides a practical, no-nonsense solution. Atmosphere is not required in utility areas: simple, inexpensive ceiling fixtures are just the thing for such locations. Plain glass globes are also useful in bathrooms, where bulbs should be totally enclosed.

In living areas central lighting remains popular because people do like a focus. But to incorporate a central light successfully, that focus must not be too bright and it should merit attention,

Left: The PH4 by Danish designer Poul Henningsen for the Danish manufacturer Louis Poulsen.

Above: The hanging light has seen a reworking in recent years, particularly by designers such as Tom Dixon (bottom right).

Right: Many Poul Henningsen designs for hanging or table lamps feature a number of overlapping "leaves" or "planes" that diffuse the light and thus avoid the problem of glare.

Hanging or pendant lights that direct most of their light upward are particularly suitable for use in living areas. Modern fixtures, such as shallow ceramic or opaque glass dishes suspended on wires, give off a soft glow at the light source itself, but bounce most of the light off the ceiling. More elaborate retro designs offer the same quality of light. Contemporary hanging lights in organic, sculptural shapes create a glowing focus of interest.

At the cheaper end of the market, there is a vast choice of shades and lanterns for pendant fixtures that completely screen the light source and create a soft glow. The paper lantern has been recently updated; colored and asymmetric forms are now available as well as the standard sphere. Similar shapes in luminously colored wrapped silk add a bohemian touch.

Pendants that direct most of their light downward, such as the familiar metal cone, work best in situations where there is a horizontal surface to bounce the light off, such as a dining table. Wide-dish pendants should be fitted with silvered-bowl bulbs to prevent glare; more versatile are narrower opaque shades in

Left: An antique pendant is hung off-center over a study area. With light shimmering off hundreds of glass beads, such a design is an undoubted attention seeker.

contributing to the decorative mood or style of the room. It should not be the only light in the room, but used in conjunction with various angled lights and lights at lower levels. Ideally, a fixed ceiling light should direct most of its light up or gently diffuse it to create a soft glow.

Alternatively, a simple way of moving away from a central arrangement, if you are stuck with the ceiling molding, is simply to lengthen the cord and suspend the light from a cup hook screwed into the ceiling in another part of the room. This strategy can be used to move a pendant, for example, from a central position to a place where it directly highlights a tabletop.

Central and hanging lights come in all styles and price brackets, including everything from basic ceiling-mounted globes through countless designs of pendant fixtures and, at the luxury end of the range, crystal chandeliers. And, of course, there can be few households that have not had recourse at some time or another to that cheap and cheerful lighting stopgap, the paper lantern.

Right: The deep bell-like shade of this reclaimed metal pendant serves to conceal the light source from direct view. Such simple, functional fixtures are widely available from salvage yards and similar sources.

Again, there are many designs on the market. Scaled-down versions of period styles can look cheap and nasty; reinterpretations of the basic theme offer more interest and integrity. Simple chandeliers based on Scandinavian or Shaker models and made of humble materials such as pewter and tin make a good accompaniment to country interiors, particularly in dining areas; many of these are designed exclusively to take candles, but there are also electrified versions. In the hands of inventive contemporary designers, the chandelier has been transformed into modern art incorporating found objects, wrought metal, and colored glass, or composed of overlapping tiers of thin porcelain tiles. There are even chandeliers that offer the option of using bulbs or candlepower.

The lantern is another period piece that has undergone a contemporary revival. The traditional glass and brass lantern, a common—perhaps too common—feature of many hallways, is no longer the main stylistic blueprint. Pierced metal lanterns and lanterns inset with jewellike panels of colored glass provide a beautiful quality of decorative light with Eastern overtones.

Left and below: Electrified chandeliers and pendant bowls are common traditional designs for hanging lights. The ceiling rose, an architectural detail found in many period homes, often looks redundant without an accompanying light fixture.

metal or porcelain where the bulb can be more fully recessed. Many pendants come with rise-and-fall mechanisms that enable you to adjust their height and vary the effects.

Chandeliers provide an unbeatable focal point: central lighting at its most glamorous and alluring. The chandelier originated simply as a multiple candle holder, a way of introducing more light when each individual source was of limited power. The elaborate refinements, such as tiers of cut glass or crystal, had a practical purpose as well, to fracture and multiply the light further. A fine period chandelier, with hundreds of lead-crystal drops, is a truly magnificent, magical, and inspiring sight, shimmering and sparkling as the light glances off each facet.

Needless to say, few of us live in surroundings that would do justice to such a feature, but that does not mean that the basic principle of the chandelier is outdated. The chandelier sidesteps many of the inherent disadvantages of central lighting, because it is composed of many small points of light. Fitting high-watt bulbs in a chandelier misses the point. These are essentially decorative fixtures and should not be relied upon for much in the way of general illumination. As a flourish or focus, chandeliers work best where there is room enough to show them off—a generously proportioned living room, for example, or a lofty stairway.

Table lamps

Above and right: Table lamps are an essential part of most lighting schemes, providing a touch of wit, an accent of color, or simply a more human element. In many classic or contemporary designs the base provides a decorative focus (above left and right), but shades also have a role to play (above center). The lava lamp adds a splash of color and possesses kitsch appeal (above right). Modern table lamps (far right) display an interest in form, from sculptural purity to more playful, evocative shapes.

Whatever style of lighting takes your fancy, lamps are indispensable. Providing local light that is reassuring, cozy, intimate, and alluring, lamps orchestrate space by setting up a series of focal points in a room. You may light a space effectively and even dramatically without incorporating lamps in your plan, but the result will lack something of the human touch. Lamps are the essence of home lighting.

At least part of the popularity of table lamps is due to the fact they are easy to understand and even to construct. The majority consist of some form of base or stand that supports the bulb holder and bulb and contains the cord that delivers power to the source. The bulb in turn is shaded, and the shape and substance of the shade is what largely controls the quality of the light. Most shades spill some light upward, some sideways, but the greater proportion focus the light downward. The effect is a soft diffusion of light around the lamp with a brighter pool at its base. Wider shades will produce a broader spill of light.

Lampshades tend to be made in materials such as fabric, paper, cardboard, and parchment, and their relative proximity to the light source means that wattages generally cannot be high. Color will have a major impact on the overall effect, tinting the light appreciably, while texture will provide a tactile quality.

Table lamps may be discreet and plain, but more often they provide the excuse to display some style and flair. With most of the light directed downward, the base is the focus of attention, thrown into relief like a decorative object in its own right.

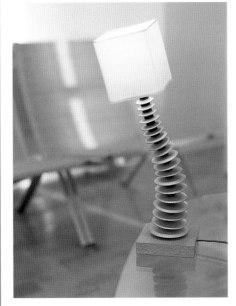

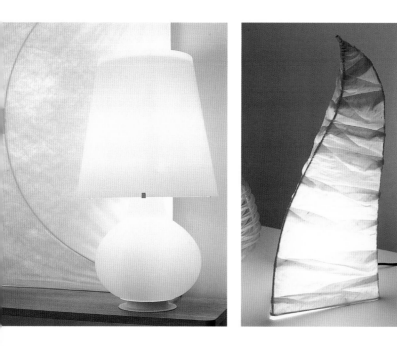

Left to right: The scale, shape, color, and material of the lampshade is integral to the overall effect of the light. Peter Wylly's innovative and influential wrapped and molded silk lights (center) combine a tactile quality with intense jewellike color. When choosing more traditional designs (left and right), it is important to visually match the size and shape of the shade to the proportions of the lamp base. The wider the base of the lampshade, the broader the spill of light will be.

Traditional models for lamp stands or bases include candlesticks, columns, vases, and urns: period flavor is a major design element. Contemporary versions generally show more of an abstraction of form. Philippe Starck's tiny Miss Sissi lamp, for example, evokes the classic café lamp, but its sleek and seamless design marks it as pure modern. Appealingly low-tech are simple table lamps that consist of no more than paper lanterns on wire stands, cheap and cheerful versions of the original (and highly priced) lights designed by the Japanese master Noguchi.

In the mass market, lamp bases are available in a vast choice of sizes, colors, textures, and materials to coordinate with every possible decorative style, from porcelain to earthenware, polished metal to glass, and rococo curlicues of wire. Bases are often sold separately from shades, which increases the already wide selection even more. Pairing a shade with a base is a question of shape and proportion as much as decorative compatibility. Wider, shallower shades are essential for large rounded bases in order to cast a large enough pool of light to clear the base all around. Slender upright supports can take smaller shades of a more compact shape. At the cutting edge of fashion, look for shades in fake fur, wrapped silk, and crushed velvet.

Left: A pair of lamps with silver gilt bases complement a more richly decorative example, whose glass base has been embellished using a technique similar to decoupage.

Right: In certain settings, simplicity works better than more elaborate designs. This reticent contemporary table lamp, with its plain metal stem and base, has a ridged glass shade that echoes the traditional pleated silk.

Floor lamps

Standard or floor-standing lamps share many of the characteristics of table lamps, but they have suffered from a dowdy and old-fashioned image in recent years, and variety is consequently much more limited.

There are indications, however, that this is beginning to change. For good reason: standing lights combine the attractions of high-level or eye-level lighting with portability and flexibility, so you are not committed to a static furniture arrangement. In addition, tall lights are not only an effective way of delivering local light to an armchair or sofa—they also help to break up the horizontal emphasis that dominates in many living areas where furniture and lighting all occupy the same relentless level.

Contemporary versions of the traditional standard-lamp format include simple, minimally detailed stands supporting crumpled paper shades, understated glass ovoids, organic or asymmetrical molded plastic forms, and overscaled Noguchi-style lanterns.

Left and right: The standard or floorstanding lamp has changed in recent years. Gone are the tasseled, fringed silk shades sitting slightly askew on ornate brass stands. They have been replaced by sleek and elegant styles, both new designs and modern classics, fashioned from glass, plastic and metal. These glamorous lamps punctuate contemporary interiors like stylish signposts of light.

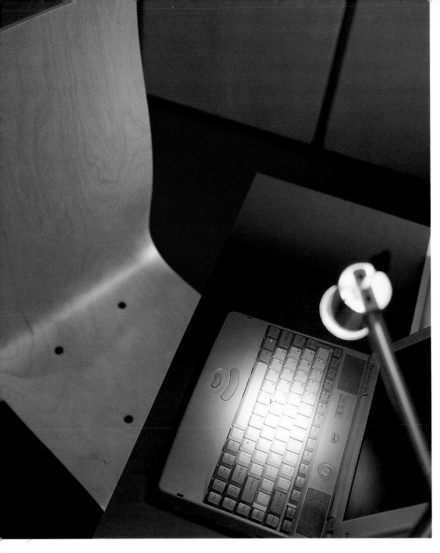

Task lights

What lighting designers call task lights, the rest of us know as desk or reading lamps. Choosing a task light should be undertaken with function firmly in mind: these types of light are not purely decorative—they are designed to help you work.

Task lights focus a high level of illumination directly where it is needed, whether this is on a page of work, a book, a drawing or a computer keyboard. To this end, the light should be fully directional, with no seepage from the top or sides. By targeting the light at the work surface, task lights avoid the problem of glare reflecting off other surfaces, for example, a computer screen. The boost in light levels is essential for all tasks that require concentration and attention to detail.

The classic task light is the goosenecked Anglepoise, invented by George Carwardine, a British automobile engineer, in 1934. Versions of the original design are still in production today. The Anglepoise, with its jointed sprung arm, is both stable and flexible, two key characteristics for a successful task light. The opaque metal shade can be angled and swiveled to prevent glare from the bulb, and the arm extends high enough to provide

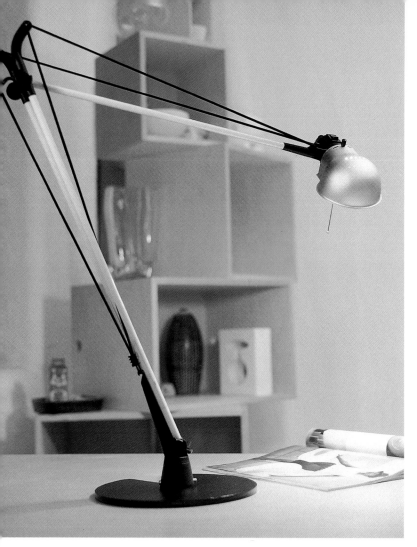

illumination over a wide area and low enough to focus a pool of light on the work at hand. It is available with a standard solid base or a clamp for securing it to the edge of the desk or worktable, a practical, space-saving feature.

Task lights come in all shapes, forms, and sizes. Some are designed to take incandescent bulbs; others halogen or fluorescent. Most incorporate some degree of flexibility, and arms may be goosenecked, cantilevered, jointed, or tensioned. At the cheapest end of the line are simple lamps on short flexible stems, generally available in a wide choice of different colors. While such models are eminently affordable, their lack of height can lead to problems with shadows and restricted light distribution. More expensive are elegant design classics such as the Bestlite or Richard Sapper's Tizio (shown on opposite page).

A step away from the modern, functional aesthetic are the established and traditional styles of desk lamp, such as the old-fashioned banker's lamp with its curved green glass shade and brass base or tole lamps with opaque shades made of metal. Suggestive of the reassuring order and respectability of the country house library or gentlemen's club, many of these are essentially decorative rather than practical.

Above left: Task lights are the workhorses of the lighting world, and most reveal their essentially utilitarian function in practical, no-nonsense design. Here, a minimal, unobtrusive desk light throws a concentrated pool of light onto a computer keyboard, preventing glare from reflecting off the screen.

Above center: Being able to adjust the height and direction of the light is an important asset when it comes to close work; fixed lighting, in this situation, would commit you to an uncomfortably static posture. Richard Sapper's classic Tizio desk lamp, designed for Artemide in 1972, has a cantilevered arm; other designs are tensioned and sprung.

Above right: Many reading and desk lamps incorporate flexible or adjustable arms that can be maneuvered into the desired position as well as a small head that can be swiveled and angled in all directions. Artemide's Cricket Tavolo, designed by Riccardo Blumer in 1991, is one such example.

Left: This minimal, businesslike desk light has a flattened triangular head that casts a wide arc of light.

Right: The most basic task lights are simple lamps with a sturdy base and bendable metal arms.

Antique and period lights

Since electric light is more than a hundred years old, early lamps and light fixtures now count as antiques. Needless to say, the finest of these are very expensive, highly collectible, and sought after; many are effectively museum pieces.

Among the most notable designers who became known for their work in this field are the American Louis Tiffany and the Frenchman Emile Gallé, both of whom produced exquisitely decorative lamps in the Art Nouveau style. The name Tiffany, in fact, has become almost a generic term for any lamp or pendant shade displaying the characteristic mosaic of leaded and colored opalescent glass. Original Tiffany lamps are superb works of art; there is a wide variety of reproductions available, with an equivalent breadth of quality.

The work of some designers, such as Charles Rennie Mackintosh, is now available in licensed reproduction, which guarantees authenticity of design. Celebrated architects such as Frank Lloyd Wright and Sir Edwin Lutyens also designed a large number of light fixtures for their interiors, and a number of these are still produced to the original designs.

Above left and center: Retro, rather than strictly "period," designs such as the Bestlite (above left) have an understated elegance that has rarely been surpassed.

Right: This superb Italian gilded metal and cut crystal wall sconce dates from the mid-nineteenth century. Chandeliers and sconces designed for candles can be electrified, but are more evocative left in their original condition.

Perhaps more deserving of the classification "retro" than "antique" are a wide range of lower-profile designs, ranging from 1930s lamp bases in the form of sinuous, reclining female figures, to rather more kitsch products of the postwar period, showing the influence of abstract art and popular culture. Second-hand shops, antique markets, and specialized dealers are good sources for all kinds of period lighting, while architectural salvage yards often have spectacular pendant and globe shades that might once have graced hotel foyers, hospitals, schools, or theaters.

Period and antique lights complement decoration with an historical flavor. However, you must make sure the light is safe to operate. If the retail outlet cannot provide guarantees, have the light checked by a professional to make sure the wiring is safe and the bulb holder and shade are compatible with modern bulbs.

Left: The innovative and acclaimed German designer Ingo Maurer is responsible for some of the most imaginative and playful of all contemporary lights. This bulb encased within a bulb is a homage to Thomas Edison.

Below: Impromptu lighting displays can be created very simply. These mini lights are individually shaded by "leaf skeletons" made of translucent fabric.

Decorative lights

Quirky, sculptural, and fun, decorative lighting is light for its own sake. You can forget all about function; these are chiefly lights that light up only themselves. The playful side of home lighting, such artful designs contribute a minimum of practical benefits but a maximum of sheer pleasure.

Tiny, beaded lamps sparkle with jewellike intensity; strange organic forms in resin glow like illuminated mushrooms; wayward wiggly shapes wrapped in silk add a calligraphic stroke of light. There are lights in the form of insects or animals, lights in the form of rockets or robots, and even flower lights—vases of plastic tulips, each individually lit from within. A recent revival of interest in 1960s and 1970s style has seen the reappearance of the lava lamp, with its hypnotic bubbling globules of color. Less tongue-in-cheek are lights that exploit the pattern of shadow to create memorable, sculptural focal points.

At the most basic level, decorative lighting can be as simple as a string of tree lights. Most people associate this type of decoration with Christmas celebrations, but tree lights can be

Center left and right:
Enchanting strings of small lanterns composed of twists of paper and tiny fabric shades around miniature bulbs add a festive air. The overall light emitted from such sources may be low, but this is more than compensated for by their atmosphere and charm.

Left: Rows of small colored glass bulbs are lit from behind by two fluorescent strips to create a light board.

Below: Ingo Maurer's witty and celebrated Bird Lamp consists of a bare bulb mounted on a brass base and connected to a scarlet cord. The minature wings are made from goose feathers.

used to create memorable effects at other times of the year. The tiny points of light emit little heat and can be used to accentuate a mantelpiece or outline a mirror or picture frame. One artist has constructed a low table from a glass-topped shallow tray filled with tree lights; for a less formal arrangement, they can be piled into a large glass container or vase without posing any risk to safety. If you want to string up tree lights outdoors, make sure you choose a weatherproof variety and use them in conjunction with a circuit breaker. Equally basic but effective are bare light bulbs painted with colorful designs.

Decorative light is particularly irresistible for children. Carousel lamps, projecting cartoon images of favorite characters, animals, planets, or stars as they revolve, transform the nightlight into a reassuring, friendly spectacle. Ceramic or glass figures lit from within have a similar appeal.

Needless to say, in the area of decorative lighting, a little can go a long way. Since light levels are generally low from such pieces, they require a darker context in which to appreciate their effect. In brightly lit surroundings or in daylight, such subtleties will simply be lost. You won't be able to read by them, or see much by them, but that is not the point. Every home should include at least some expression of the sheer joy and artistry of light.

Living *with* light

Successful lighting depends on acquainting yourself with the characteristics of different light sources and the choice of fixtures, how they function, and what they can and cannot do. But the final, and most important, part of the equation is the environment in which the lights will be used.

Lighting is a critical element of interior decoration, and to maximize its potential a lighting plan must be considered in conjunction with other decorative and functional parameters. You can't decide how to light until you know what you are going to light. There is a practical, as well as aesthetic, side to the issue. Once you've decorated, it can be disheartening to discover that you should have incorporated mounted or recessed light fixtures, or cannot plug in a lamp where you need one. Cutting holes in the ceiling, adding new outlets or hiding wires in wallboard are not major disruptions, but they can be painful when the paintwork is almost pristine.

In a perfect world, we would all be accomplished designers of our own interiors, able to start with a blank page and carry our plans logically through to completion. In reality, most of us fall short of that ideal, being more inclined to learn from previous mistakes or identify problems after, rather than before, they've arisen. And instead of a blank page, we tend to find ourselves dealing with spaces that satisfy some of our needs and tastes, but not others.

If this is the case, remember that alterations to lighting, at any stage, can radically improve the quality of your space. The temptation to stay with the status quo may be great, but for less expense than a new sofa and less disruption than new flooring, new lighting can transform your home. But before you design or choose a new lighting plan, it is essential that you first turn to pages 172–175 to review the practical issues involved and to learn how to analyze your own personal requirements.

Lighting can be broadly categorized into four different types according to function—ambient, task, accent, and information. Just as there are few areas in the home that can be lit solely by one fixture, there are also few areas that do not require a combination of these different types of lighting. Unlike decorating, where it is perfectly possible, although it may be somewhat dull, to come up with one basic plan and apply it throughout an interior, there is no one single solution to lighting that is able to serve every purpose or need. Every room in the home requires individual consideration with respect to lighting.

Types of lighting

Different activities take place in different parts of different rooms, and each of these activities is likely to require different lighting. To make sure the lighting within a room meets all the demands that is placed upon it, lighting designers separate lighting into four different categories—ambient, task, accent, and information. A successful lighting plan will always use a combination of the four different types of light to create an interior where working practicality is coupled with richness of visual experience.

A good lighting plan has nothing to do with adding a downlight here or a table lamp there or changing the shade of the hall pendant. Such minor alterations may be beneficial, but the most effective and successful lighting plans stem from a well-considered and coherent plan that addresses all the characteristics and meets all the demands of a particular space by utilizing each of the four different types of lighting. Most of the rooms in a house have complex lighting requirements, arising out of the wide variety of functions they serve, and therefore they demand a high degree of flexibility together with attention to aesthetics

and style. Only a few areas, principally utility rooms such as workshops, garages, or laundry rooms, can be lit simply and effectively by one type of lighting alone.

A successful lighting plan should also take into account how the areas in the home are linked together. Abrupt changes in light levels can be disorienting and even dangerous if you are dazzled or cast into relative darkness as you move from one room to the next. Achieving a balance between variety in the style and effect of lighting, and a sense of coherence and progression, is important when you come to put it all together.

Above: This small, brushed aluminum table lamp, designed to take a 25-watt bulb, provides some local light but largely serves as a point of interest.

Left: An aluminum spotlight on an accordion arm is wall-mounted over kitchen shelving to provide flexible and adjustable task light for a preparation area and counter.

Ambient lighting

Also known as general or background lighting, ambient light is the light we see by. All rooms or areas in the home where we live and work require ambient lighting. Ambient light is the direct substitute or supplement for natural light; it makes interiors visible. It is commonly supplied by fixtures that diffuse light over surfaces such as walls and ceilings or that glow omnidirectionally. At the same time, ambient light can be said to be the sum of light in an interior. A series of task or work lights, for example, may generate enough light within a space to raise the general light level effectively and constitute ambient lighting in themselves.

In terms of creating atmosphere, ambient light needs to be partnered with more local light, accenting decoration or focusing on specific areas, in order to generate moody contrasts of light and shade. On its own, it can be bland and featureless.

Right and below right: Ambient light is most effectively supplied by a variety of sources, such as pendant lights combined with standing lamps or recessed downlights combined with concealed track lighting.

Above: Cut into the thickness of the wall, a narrow recess with architectural tube lights is an unusual but strikingly effective way of providing background illumination.

Far right: An industrial-style bulkhead wall fixture combines with pendant lights and more local task lighting to supplement the flood of natural light streaming in through the large expanse of windows.

Task lighting

Task lighting is lighting that allows a specific purpose or activity to be carried out efficiently, safely, and comfortably. Most task lights are directional and local in their effect, from the reading lamp angled over the desk to the downlight over the kitchen counter. Positioning is therefore critical, and sources should remain invisible to eliminate glare.

Task lights can double as practical and ambient sources of light: a table lamp positioned by the bedside can provide enough light for reading in bed as well as a soft source of background illumination. Generally, however, since task lights cast a bright directional beam, they tend to create sharp contrasts of light and shade, which can be tiring and uncomfortable.

Above: Each of these elegant wall-mounted Bestlites, here used as bedside reading lights, has its own dimmer control. This is a versatile and practical treatment that permits varying mood control within a bedroom and allows one partner enough light to read by while the other dozes.

Above left: Small, unobtrusive downlights are discreetly recessed in the underside of wall-mounted kitchen cabinets to provide plenty of local task light for the counters.

Left: A desk lamp should be positioned so light falls on the page or keyboard, ideally from the right if you are right-handed, or vice versa if you are left-handed. Some additional background light is usually a good idea to prevent tiring extremes of brightness and shadow. Here a concealed light source behind a floor-level window shade serves the purpose.

Accent lighting

Accent lighting is low-level, focused light targeted at decorative features of the interior—a collection of glass, a piece of sculpture, a painting, architectural detail. Spotlights of various beam widths are commonly used as accent light, but other forms of directional light can have the same impact. A floor-level uplight placed behind a large leafy plant will create a focus of interest by casting a pattern of shadows over the walls and ceiling. Ideally, accent lighting should be discreet and relatively low level. The aim is to focus attention on what you're illuminating, not the light itself, but that illumination should not be too bright and dazzling or it will upset the fine balance of the overall lighting plan.

Right: A shallow curved niche in a hall is transformed into a dramatic display area by concealed downlighting.

Below: The pattern, color, and texture of lampshades are intensified when the light is switched on, creating a decorative accent through very simple means.

Decorative lighting also falls into this category, including those lights that emit only enough illumination to highlight their own shape and form—if they throw a little local light, it is an added bonus. Accent lighting also includes the warm and flattering light cast by the "natural" sources of firelight and candlelight. In such cases it is the light itself that provides the accent or focus of interest.

Intensely evocative, beguiling, characterful, and atmospheric, accent lighting makes an important aesthetic and stylistic contribution to any lighting plan.

Below: Backlighting intriguing objects adds a sense of drama to an interior. Accent lighting leans heavily on theatrical techniques to create a sense of occasion.

Information lighting

Information lighting provides on-the-spot light to enable us to negotiate our way safely or pick out critical signposts. The light inside the closet or refrigerator, the light over the doorbell or beside the front door, the approach light triggered by movement are all examples of information lighting. Information lighting can also be used to create striking architectural statements. Floor-level lights inset on stairs or at the base of walls can create dramatic lit pathways that enhance structure and form.

Above left: Low-level recessed wall lights provide unobtrusive yet effective information lighting for a stairway landing.

Above: This path of light lends importance to the entrance of a home as well as allowing the drive to be negotiated safely.

Right: A series of recessed wall lights is positioned so light grazes each stair tread and riser.

Left: In a tiny internal courtyard, matching wall lights illuminate a large mirror cleverly placed to increase the sense of space.

The visual appearance of a lamp or light fixture may not be not the most important factor when it comes to achieving a good quality of light, but it is far from being an irrelevance. From paint finishes to pillow covers, wallpaper to curtains, style is our natural expression of taste and individuality. A light, while it is essentially a piece of equipment designed for a particular purpose, should also make a contribution to the decorative character of the home. And, just like any other decorative element, lights offer an exciting opportunity to explore the potential of color, texture, and form.

Lighting the home with style

In terms of style, lamps, and light fixtures can be loosely categorized as traditional or contemporary. Traditional lights, such as chandeliers, table and floor lamps, sconces, and pendants, generally recall in their design earlier forms of artificial lighting, such as candles, gasoliers, and oil lamps, or display a strong decorative element that is to some extent historical in flavor. Contemporary lights range from the discreet and minimal to freer, more sculptural forms with no stylistic antecedents. Within these two broad camps there is a huge range of colors, materials, and designs from which to choose.

Traditional styles of light are naturally at home in period surroundings; contemporary designs in modern interiors. Most of us will instinctively avoid the obvious anomalies, eschewing ruffled lampshades and ornate sconces where the look is one of hard-edged simplicity, or the defiant technicality of track lighting and modern task lights where the emphasis is on the ornate and antique. But rules are made to be broken, and lights can also be the vehicle for effective stylistic contrasts. In a sleek, pared-down space, with minimal furnishing, a decorative or traditional style of light, such as a chandelier, can make a striking focal point. Similarly, concealed modern fixtures can bring a new quality of light to traditional interiors and provide a welcome breathing space where much of the lighting is more eye-catching and decorative.

Lights that are coordinated stylistically with the rest of the decor in a room create a sense of unity and coherence; lights that make a contrast add the vitality of accent. To avoid either a numbing uniformity or an overly hectic effect, you need a bit of both.

Above: In an interior that displays a strong period flavor in detailing and furnishings, real candlelight provides an authentic sense of historical character.

Left: A sinuously curved brass floor lamp, with a pleated silk shade, makes an elegant accompaniment to a daybed. Style is not always an issue, but in certain circumstances the appearance of the fixture assumes additional importance.

Color is a critical element. Lamp bases and shades that are matched to the dominant shades of a color scheme can result in a soothing and well-considered look, but there is always a risk that you may decide to paint your walls rather sooner than you wish to replace your lamps. A better solution might be to combine a number of lamps that are essentially neutral in tone with one or two that provide a vibrant splash of color in an interior.

Texture adds a material dimension. In a room where there is a great deal of fabric and soft furnishing, lampshades and bases or stands made of hard, glossy or reflective materials, such as porcelain, glass, and metal, sharpen up the visual edge. Basic natural materials, such as paper, wood, and pottery, are more sympathetic in simple or rustic rooms where the emphasis is on the elemental qualities of different surfaces.

Scale and form are also important. Lamps on wiggly wire or curly metal stands add a calligraphic touch. Large bases and shades or large-scale photographer's lamps provide a sense of drama, while tiny jewellike lamps transform odd corners into intimate focal points. Playing around with contrasts of shape and proportion introduces an element of surprise, a twist of wit and humor that keeps interiors from looking too safe and predictable.

The basic principles of good lighting that were discussed on pages 27–43 apply throughout the interior, and it is well worth reviewing these principles before you read on. Try to keep them in mind and, above all, remember that light is an aid to experience and activity, and keep your attention focused on the functional purposes that each space must fulfill.

Above right: A diffusion of soft ambient lighting comes from the combination of a simple table lamp with a backlit panel of fabric stretched over a metal framework.

Above center: The translucent white shade and urn-shaped base of this traditional lamp is complemented by a large glass vase of white flowers.

Above far right: This darker, more opaque shade throws much of the light downward, illuminating the lamp base.

Right: A window seat is made even more inviting by a wall-mounted lamp that provides local light for reading.

Center: The shape and opacity of this Japanese-style light concentrates light downward.

Far right: A brass library light on an elbow-jointed arm provides flexible bedside lighting.

Lighting halls and stairs

The entrance to your home raises the curtain on what is to follow. The point of welcome and departure for guests and the mediating zone between indoors and out, the hall is the focus of what architects like to call "circulation space"—in other words, the connecting areas of the interior that we move through *en route* to somewhere else. Lighting is a key factor in emphasizing this sense of progression, leading the eye on and easing the transition from the public realm of the street to the privacy of the home.

The hall is not really a room at all, in the sense of a place where we spend much time. And it is rarely proportioned as such; most halls are long and narrow, with a restricted floor area and very little in the way of existing features. There is likely to be little or no room for furniture, although the walls may offer opportunities for display. All of these factors impose certain limitations on the lighting. At the same time, however, lighting may be one of the few ways in which you can generate a sense of character and distinction without compromising the existing space.

Left: Branched wall lights provide good background illumination in a hall, reflecting on the painted woodwork and polished floor. An antique ceiling light adds a decorative flourish.

Right: On staircases, there is a risk that low-level pendants and wall-mounted uplights may dazzle those ascending or descending. Here, discreet yet effective floor-level lighting safely illuminates a narrow flight of steps.

Above, left to right: Floor-level lighting is a dramatic but highly practical way of illuminating halls, staircases, and other circulation areas. Downlights (center) make sense in areas of the home where flexible arrangement is not practical.

Above: The transforming effect of lighting is demonstrated in these comparative day and night views. By day, the glazed corridor dissolves the boundary between interior and exterior spaces, bringing natural light into the heart of the house. By night, the entire window wall becomes a light panel, forming a dramatic backdrop to the landscape design.

Ceiling or wall lights make obvious sense in the hall. Recessed downlights accentuate the path from the front door through to the rest of the home; wall-mounted uplights create a sense of drama and architectural distinction. If the hall is used as a place of display, with pictures lining the walls, spotlights or track lighting can be angled to focus the attention. If the hall is wide enough, a small lamp on a narrow table or shelf near the entrance will add a warm note of hospitality. And pendant lights, provided they are not suspended too low, are also a good solution, particularly if they contribute a decorative touch in their own right. The sweep of a stair, descending to a hall, can be marked by an eye-catching design such as a chandelier or colored-glass lantern. However, you must make sure the light looks just as good from above as from below, or those coming down the stairs will either be treated to an unlovely view or blinded by glare.

Pendant and wall lights are ideal solutions for stairways; top lighting gives definition to stair edges and reduces the risk of accidental tumbles. Using the same fixtures in the hall and up the

stairs lends a sense of unity and coherence. Striking contemporary effects can be achieved by recessing tiny lights into the base of a wall or into stair treads to create a glowing pathway that heightens architectural drama.

Don't forget to make the most of natural light. Fanlights or glazed panels in doors, both exterior and interior, will help to spread light from bright areas to darker, more enclosed rooms. More evocative, even magical, effects can be achieved with panes of colored or etched glass, while a skylight set into the roof at the apex of a stairwell will generate a feeling of light and airy expansiveness. A strategically placed mirror will also bring added depth and sparkle, multiplying the available light in a space.

When lighting halls and stairs, there are a number of practical points to remember. Positioning a switch near the front door will prevent you from having to enter a dark house. In the same way, switches should be located at strategic places on each level of the staircase. It is essential to avoid the potential hazard of trailing wires that might trip people. Floor-standing lights can be an obstruction if the floor area is restricted, and table lamps risk being knocked over as people pass by. Glare can be a problem. Low-level pendants can cause glare at eye level, and angled lighting must be correctly positioned to avoid dazzling those coming down the stairs or through the front door. Finally, install a dimmer switch to accommodate variations in natural light levels and help the eye adapt to the transition between indoors and out.

Lighting living rooms

Living rooms present the greatest challenge to the lighting designer, amateur or professional. Serving as both a place for general relaxation and as a catchall for activities that cannot be accommodated elsewhere, the living room in the contemporary home is the quintessential multipurpose space. At the same time, the living room carries the burden of our stylistic and decorative aspirations. It must look good enough to impress friends and neighbors, or at least satisfy our own desire for personal expression—style is an issue that cannot be sidestepped.

On the practical side, living rooms often play host to a variety of disparate activities, united only by the fact that there is nowhere else for them to take place. Watching television, reading books, listening to music, and entertaining friends are all standard living-room pursuits, but in many households, the living room may also

Right and below: A room with a view. Constantly changing and immensely appealing, natural light enhances a sense of well-being. The enormous unscreened windows on two sides of this Manhattan apartment flood the living room with light and provide views of one of the most exciting cityscapes in the world.

be where children play or do homework, or where hobbies and concentrated work are undertaken. There may also be a dining area sharing the same space. At least some of these activities will require specific task lighting or directional local light for them to be performed comfortably and effectively.

On the aesthetic side, lighting should be planned to complement and enhance both the existing spatial quality of the room and the style of decoration. There may be objects or pictures that deserve to be accented, architectural features to emphasize, dominant colors or textures that require a sympathetic quality of light.

Reconciling these two sides, the practical and the aesthetic, requires a sensitive combination of three of the main types of lighting: ambient, task, and accent. Flexibility is the order of the day. Lifestyles change, as do interests and activities, redefining the functions living areas must fulfill. Tastes change, too, and the living room is likely to undergo a succession of stylistic makeovers as well as different arrangements of furniture. For these reasons, it is generally best to avoid nonflexible types of lighting, such as downlighting, which will restrict your future options unnecessarily. Ambient lighting can be better achieved using floor and table lamps and freestanding uplights, which can be moved as needed. Movable spotlights on tracks also allow for repositioning. If you

do wish to install stationary lighting, it is best aligned with a permanent feature. Wall lights, for example, can be positioned in alcoves or flanking a fireplace, rather than at either end of a sofa that you may want to move at a later date.

Table and floor lamps are especially effective in living rooms. They enclose seating areas in intimate circles of light and generate a sense of movement between different parts of the room. Lamps at different heights also break up the strong horizontal bias of furnishings. Equally important, the family of table and floor lamps is so stylistically varied that it is easy to coordinate designs and colors with the overall decorating scheme.

The presence of a central ceiling light poses something of a problem in many living rooms. In period homes, where the outlet may be encircled by decorative plasterwork, removing the light completely can look odd, yet equally redundant is the strategy of hanging a pendant from the center and never switching it on. One solution is to choose a decorative fixture that provides an attractive focus in its own right, and light it with low-wattage bulbs so it does not create an overpowering central focus. Alternatively, extend the cord of the light and suspend it either low over a coffee table or from another part of the room entirely. Simple large-scale lanterns often look good treated this way.

Living room lighting should enhance the finer points of the room's structure and help to correct less desirable features. If the room is small, use uplighting to increase the sense of space by bouncing diffused light off walls and ceilings. This sense of expansiveness can be increased if furnishings are moved a short distance out from the walls and uplights are positioned behind them. If the ceiling is painted white or a light tone, uplighting will have the effect of making the wall color less dominant and enveloping; if the ceiling has interesting architectural features, such as moldings or beams, uplighting will also bring these to the fore.

On the other hand, uplighting can make a large room seem cavernous and intimidating in scale. The answer in this case is to opt for more localized lighting effects with lamps and angled spots, so the room appears as a series of interconnected spaces.

The living room is the ideal location for purely decorative lighting, and this element is especially important in contemporary settings where lights are generally discreet in appearance or concealed from view. Without the humanizing touch of decorative light, even the most stylish living room can seem a little austere. Firelight and candlelight add an almost spiritual dimension, while lights that are beautiful objects in their own right create focal points. Tiny points of sparkling accent light generate a sense of vitality.

Above far left: Living room lighting should be flexible enough to cater to a number of different moods and activities. Here, discreet recess-mounted downlights combine with more dramatic wall-mounted sidelights to provide a good level of general illumination, while table lamps provide a more intimate focus.

Above left and right: Table and floor-standing lamps are practical and flexible additions to living-room lighting plans.

Left: A pair of brass swing-arm wall-mounted fixtures supplement natural light at each end of a broad and inviting window seat.

Right: A pair of chrome floor-standing lamps of varying heights make neat punctuation points beside a fireplace. The small shades on top of the long stems make a play of scale.

Below: An undisputed lighting classic, Isamu Noguchi's beehive light sculpture has inspired many imitators. Recalling the simplicity of Eastern hanging lanterns made of paper, the scale of the piece adds to its impact.

Above: A Peter Wylly light bridges the gap between light and sculpture. Silvered-bowl bulbs mounted on a suspended plastic spiral provide a new take on the fixed central focus.

Left: The lava lamp adds an accent of color and humor to a corner of this sleek contemporary living room.

In rooms where people often gather together to celebrate, the "natural" sources of candlelight and firelight are especially poignant and meaningful. Neither of these sources of light is particularly strong, so for maximum impact it is best to dim artificial lights down low. Both candles and fires produce a warm and flattering light that is both highly sympathetic for skin tones and psychologically reassuring. What is more, this moving light—the flicker of a candle or flames dancing in the hearth—has a calming, almost mesmeric effect.

As far as light sources are concerned, incandescent is most people's preferred choice for living room lighting. Inherently warm and hospitable, soothing and cozy, incandescent light projects all those emotional qualities that we most associate with relaxation and comfort. The cooler and crisper tones of halogen can also be effective in small doses of sparkling accent light, where it gives extra clarity to color, texture, and form.

It should go without saying that living room lighting should be dimmable. In the evocative theatrical phrase describing the moment when the house lights go down, dimming is "turning on the night." Varying light levels will let you respond to the moods and demands of different occasions and times of day. You may need several circuits to provide optimum flexibility and control.

If you read in your living room, you will need concentrated light on the page. Excessively bright light, however, will create too great a contrast between what you are reading and your surroundings, which can cause eyestrain. The ideal position for a reading light is to one side, slightly above and behind your chair. A lamp or light in this position will illuminate the page directly without casting shadows. Table lamps, task lights, floor lamps, and angled spotlights (provided they are not too bright) are all suitable for the purpose.

We may pretend we don't, or wish we didn't, but many of us spend a good deal of our time in the living room watching television. It is essential to provide the right lighting conditions for comfortable viewing. As our parents often warned us, watching television in the dark is bad for the eyes. The reasons are obvious. Television is a light source. Images on the screen are constantly moving, demanding equivalent shifts in focus. If no additional light is

Above: Candlelight is warm, flattering, and lively— an unbeatable source of atmosphere in living areas. The perfect accompaniment to celebrations and gatherings, the effect is too enjoyable to be restricted to special occasions.

Left: Custom-designed wall fixtures conceal the light source while washing the wall above and below. The simple box design works well with the built-in shelving.

Above right: A pair of striking antique lamps provide decorative impact. The nineteenth-century wrought-iron "bouquets" are set in fake stone bases; the shades are pierced parchment.

supplied, there is a risk of headache as the eye struggles to accommodate the contrast between the dark room and the bright box in the corner of it. At the same time, if the light in the room is too bright, it is hard to see the television clearly. During the day, for example, natural light from a window can dim the picture on the screen to near-invisibility. Ideally, there should be a light beside or behind the television that reduces the contrast between the screen and the rest of the room, supplemented by a low level of diffused ambient light. If a light is too close to the television, the screen may be obscured by reflection, and the same is true of lights placed behind the viewer or between the viewer and the set.

The living room is where we put our best foot forward, decoratively speaking, and in many cases this means display. Pictures, glassware, objects, and books take pride of place, inviting our appreciation of color, texture, and form. Without sympathetic and appropriate lighting, such possessions lose much of their fascination and impact. Inspiration for accent lighting can come from museum and retail displays. Low-voltage halogen lights are perfect for accenting decorative objects with tiny points of light, and are discreet enough to work in the context of traditionally decorated rooms as well as contemporary settings. Spotlights and eyeball downlights have a more overt presence, but can be angled to target whatever you want to emphasize.

The positioning or direction of accent light is critical. Downlighting creates a sense of drama that isolates an object in space rather like a museum exhibit. Lighting from below and behind will throw an object into mysterious silhouette, while light angled from the side will reveal texture and form. To maximize the sparkling transparency of glass, light should be directed from below or behind. Spots or fluorescent tubes concealed within the base of a display cabinet or behind a baffle underneath glass shelving can be particularly effective. Clip-on spots, angled to graze light across shelving, will turn storage into a feature while facilitating the selection of books, CDs, or cassettes.

Pictures in particular require sensitive lighting. Without any specific illumination, pictures and paintings can lose much of their impact after nightfall, but inappropriate lighting is almost worse than no light at all. The light must be angled correctly, so as not to cause glaring reflections on the picture glass or the glossy texture of an oil painting, and it should light the entire picture area evenly. Spotlights provide a targeted light, while eyeball downlights create a broader wash of illumination. Special picture lights that extend on narrow arms over the top of the painting are the traditional option. To be effective, the fixture should extend the full width of the picture and project far enough out from the wall to cast light evenly from top to bottom.

Lighting kitchens

Increasingly, the kitchen is performing a dual role. As the hardest-working area in the home, where food is stored, prepared, cooked, and served on a daily basis, the kitchen demands efficient lighting at fairly bright levels to allow tasks to be carried out comfortably and safely. At the same time, the kitchen has become much more of a general living area, a place where the family tends to congregate between as well as during mealtimes. As in the living room, or other multipurpose areas, reconciling the practical lighting requirements with the more emotional, aesthetic side requires careful consideration.

In the bad old days, kitchen lighting often began and ended with a central fluorescent strip, an arrangement that ultimately proved as impractical as it was depressing. True, fluorescent light is long-lasting, economical, and bright but, installed in a central position and unshaded, it casts a sickly pallor over the entire kitchen, an effect more clinical than hospitable. Furthermore, such lighting, while delivering an adequate level of background illumination, cannot be targeted where you need it most. Fluorescent, particularly the warmer varieties, can have a role in kitchen lighting, but it should not be the dominant light source.

Above: Open-plan kitchen areas call for versatile lighting arrangements. The row of pendants over the table provide atmospheric background light, while downlighting over work surfaces allows more detailed work to take place.

Left: Interior lighting in a kitchen wall cabinet facilitates storage and retrieval. Glossy metal surfaces reflect the light.

Right: Tiny halogen downlights recessed above and below cabinets provide efficient and utterly discreet task lighting.

When planning lighting for kitchens, it is best to begin with the functional requirements, adding more decorative or local light once the practicalities have been addressed. Most kitchens contain some fixed or built-in elements; some are entirely built in. Even so-called "unfitted" kitchens, composed of freestanding cupboards, hutches, and butcher blocks, have an inherent stability of layout determined by the servicing of plumbing and electricity. These static points—sinks, ovens, and stoves—provide the blueprint for a lighting plan. Unlike living rooms, where the emphasis is on flexibility, kitchens are the ideal location for stationary types of lighting, such as downlights and ceiling-mounted spots, since the basic arrangement of cabinets and appliances can be assumed to be more or less permanent.

Aside from the essentially built-in nature of many kitchens, there are other factors that argue in favor of built-in, mounted, or recessed forms of lighting. Pendants can sometimes result in high-level glare. Freestanding light fixtures or lamps can obstruct the floorspace or clutter counters and shelves that should be kept clear for storage, cooking, and preparation. Similarly, trailing cords can be a hazard at floor or counter level, where they run the risk of either tripping someone or coming into contact with extreme heat or water, while sockets that are already required for

Above far left: Uplights concealed at the top of these cabinets bounce light off the ceiling for good background illumination, while concealed downlights under the units target the main work surface.

Below far left: Fluorescent tubes, installed vertically behind frosted glass panels, have a cool, modern look.

Left: Dimmable downlights behind the screen of glass panels to one side of this kitchen provide soft ambient light. Low-voltage halogen lights accentuate the working part of the kitchen, while framing spotlights target specific points of interest.

Above: Pendants provide good levels of ambient light while downlights target counters.

powering appliances may be overloaded if you also use them to plug in a light. And, last, prominent fixtures can attract a build-up of dust and grease even in the best-run households.

Kitchens require good ambient light of a fairly high level combined with task light for the working areas. The overall effect should be as free of shadow and glare as possible. Safety is a prime consideration. Even the preparation of an ordinary meal involves many potentially dangerous procedures: using sharp implements and working in close proximity to steam, boiling water, gas flames, or glowing rings. If you attempt to cook in a dimly lit area, the risks are obvious, but dazzling glare can also be a problem. Good lighting, both in the sense of adequate levels and proper positioning, and in terms of color rendering, is also essential when you are reading a recipe or endeavoring to present food in as attractive a way as possible.

For general or ambient light, make use of the ceiling, either as a reflective plane or as a surface for mounting or recessing fixtures. Tube lights concealed behind moldings at the top of wall cupboards will wash the ceiling with light; wall-mounted spots, angled up, or wall-mounted uplights have the same effect. Downlights, particularly low-voltage halogen varieties, are ideal for general kitchen lighting. Recessed fixtures are discreet and glare-free. Spotlights can also serve as sources of ambient lighting, as can a central light if the kitchen area is very small.

Task lighting must be in accord with the basic kitchen layout, whether it is galley, L-shaped, or island in plan. The essential requirement is to light each area effectively and in such a way that you are not working in your own shadow. Light that is angled from behind as you stand at the counter, stove, or sink should be avoided. Instead, position lights so illumination comes from the front or side of the work area. Directional downlights can be used for task lighting, but they can create uncomfortable extremes of light and dark, with the counter too bright and the walls and wall units in relative darkness. More effective are wall- or ceiling-mounted spots or strip lighting concealed behind a baffle at the base of wall units. Downlights can also be recessed in the base of cabinets, while shaded task lights, such as reading lamps on folding or adjustable arms, can be mounted on the wall over the work surface or clamped to the edge of an overhead shelf.

Accent or decorative light is not essential in a kitchen. But kitchens become much more pleasant places when there is a decorative element to the display of everyday things. Rows of shiny canisters and glass storage jars merit a degree of attention, as do hanging racks of utensils and pots and pans, not to mention the colors and textures of fresh vegetables and fruit. Small accent spots can be used to highlight such arrangements. If the kitchen doubles as a dining area, accent lighting can provide a discreet background source when the main task lights are switched off.

There are a number of specialized kitchen lights that make practical additions to a plan. Many stove hoods or fan units have integral lights that illuminate the burners as the hood is pulled out or the fan activated. Some hanging rails for suspending kitchen paraphernalia incorporate lights within the design; these

Far left: Simple fixtures can be very effective for kitchen task lighting. A pair of second-hand clip-on spots combined with a wall-mounted spot on a folding arm focus light right where it is needed.

Left: Two types of different downlighting provide ambient and focused illumination. Static downlights in recesses are combined with tiny low-voltage directional downlights that shine a narrow glare-free beam over the kitchen island.

Right: Many kitchen manufacturers supply their own light fixtures. This robust downlight is designed to be mounted under the surface of wall-hung cabinets.

can be very effective over island units or central worktables. For large cupboards or pantries, interior lights triggered by the opening of the door, like the lights in refrigerators, are very useful.

As far as light sources are concerned, low-voltage halogen scores very highly in kitchens, where its crisp white light is both practical and aesthetically pleasing. Halogen aids color differentiation, which is useful when you are examining produce, assessing how well food is cooked, or making judgments about presentation and display. But the whiteness of the light is also complementary to many kitchen materials and surfaces—the sleek sheen of chrome and stainless steel, the transparency of glass, and the gleaming white finish of appliances. In more rustic surroundings, where surfaces and finishes have the earthier appeal of scrubbed pine and terra-cotta, incandescent sources can be more sympathetic.

Due to its poor color rendering, fluorescent is not ideal when it comes to kitchen aesthetics. However, it can be a practical means of task lighting if the source is shaded or concealed. The solution is to combine it with other, truer light sources and opt for the varieties that are somewhat warmer in tone.

Dimming is not a priority for kitchens that are used solely for cooking, but in the case of multipurpose spaces, it provides a useful way of changing the focus from the working part of the room to the eating or relaxing area. Similarly, accent lights or small lamps perched on a shelf or at the corner of a hutch, for example, provide more atmospheric light when the mood alters. As in other areas where different activities are accommodated, more than one circuit may be required for optimum flexibility, allowing you to control ambient and task lighting separately.

A good quality of light is also essential for the unhurried enjoyment of food. It is small wonder that fast-food outlets rely on harsh, bright light bouncing off hard, shiny surfaces to make sure the turnover of customers is as rapid as possible. Conversely, restaurants where the comfort and pleasure of the clientele comes first and foremost often display some of the most theatrical, imaginative, and intriguing of all lighting arrangements.

Some restaurants, especially those that are situated below street level, or where there is no direct access to natural light, employ highly sophisticated lighting schemes to make sure the light levels in the space change according to the time of day. Using photocells and time clocks controlled by a computer, subtle adjustments in light are programmed to mimic the changing pattern of natural light as the day progresses or the seasons change. The result is a responsive quality of light that generates specific moods for different occasions.

Right and below: Lighting track permits different types of light fixture to be powered from the same supply. In this modern kitchen, individual spotlights for general and accent lighting are combined with pendant spots hung low over tables.

Lighting dining areas

The dining room as a separate entity is an endangered species, one that is fast disappearing from contemporary homes. Demands on space and the relaxed informality of modern entertaining, not to mention the flexibility of family mealtimes, means that we increasingly tend to eat in part of a room that is largely devoted to another purpose. There are living-dining areas and kitchen-dining areas and even kitchen-living-dining areas, but the dining room itself is far less common than it was.

The challenge when it comes to lighting a dining area often centers on the need to provide more or less instant atmosphere and intimacy within the context of an open-plan or multipurpose space. However relaxed we have become about etiquette and convention, sharing a meal together with family and friends is still regarded as a special occasion that demands relaxing, sympathetic, and often celebratory lighting.

Above: In a sparsely furnished contemporary dining area, numerous tangled strands of dimmed white Christmas lights are woven around a wire sphere to create a deconstructed chandelier. Additional glass shapes suspended from the sphere sparkle with reflected light.

Lighting a dining area in the home is naturally far less complex. But it is nevertheless worth bearing in mind that the lighting will have to be flexible enough to suit different times of the day. What may be appropriate for Sunday breakfast with the papers, for example, will not provide the right atmosphere for an intimate dinner for two or a special family celebration.

Lighting for dining areas begins with the table. We eat with our eyes, as the saying goes, and food is always more appetizing when we can appreciate the colors and textures of what is on the plate. At the same time, really bright light works against the sense of intimacy and enclosure that makes a hospitable gathering. Lighting should focus attention on the table and help make eating a shared and enjoyable experience.

Pendants, from simple metal shades to chandeliers, are the mainstay of dining room lighting. Directing a broad spread of light down on the table, a pendant provides both enough ambient light to see by and a cozy focused circle that draws people together. The light source itself should not be too bright. A white tablecloth, sparkling glasses and flatware, and the glazed sheen of porcelain or pottery will all act to reflect the light gently upward, illuminating the faces of those seated around the table.

A pendant should hang low enough over the table not to cause glare from the light source, but it should not be so low that it interferes with views and conversation across the table. Pendants with rise-and-fall mechanisms allow you to play around with positioning, but once you have determined the optimum level, this degree of flexibility is of little further benefit.

The level of the pendant is obviously a key factor in avoiding glare, but the shape of the pendant can also have an impact. Deeper shades, where the bulb is recessed within the fixture, are better than shallower designs that leave it exposed to view. Silvered-bowl bulbs are also a good idea, since they reflect the light back onto the dish of the shade and diffuse its strength.

A long table may require a series of pendants to light its full length. Free lighting track, where fixtures can be plugged in at any position, make good sense in this situation; track also allows pendants to be combined with accent or directional spots that are angled away from the table to highlight points of interest on the walls. Free track also makes it possible for pendants to be removed if you wish to clear the space for entertaining, for example.

Downlighting, a common strategy in restaurants, can provide an atmospheric alternative to pendant lights. Positioning is critical. Downlights should be placed where they will pick out the

Far left below: Candlelight is the most atmospheric light source for dining. A hanging lantern with incandescent candle lamps provides a soft counterpoint to the real flames on the table.

Left: A floor light on a curly metal stand makes a sympathetic choice for an informal seating area.

Right: Computerized controls sited at the doorway allow fine adjustments to be made to the lighting mood in this dining room.

Below: A pendant by the Danish designer Louis Poulsen creates an intimate focus in an open-plan kitchen.

centerpiece of a table, such as a flower arrangement, or create pools of light along its length that are then softly reflected back onto faces. Downlights that are positioned directly over the heads of diners, however, will only create the uncomfortable sensation of being spotlit, as well as creating hard, unflattering shadows on the faces. Because placement is so important, downlighting is only practical in areas where the table will remain stationary.

Away from the table, gentle background lighting will mean there is not too great a contrast of light levels. Small shaded wall lights are a traditional dining room feature; these are more discreet if shades match the color of the wall. Alternatively, table lamps on sideboards or storage units, low-wattage uplights in the corners of the room, or accent lighting trained on pictures or decorative displays supplement the light from the table without skewing the focus of the room. Both the light for the table and the background lighting should be dimmable to allow you to make subtle adjustments to mood and emphasis. This is particularly important in dining areas that are used for other activities, such as studying, or that form part of a larger open-plan space.

Incandescent is undoubtedly the best light source for both people and food, rendering colors truthfully and flattering the complexion. And candles, the most flattering and intimate light of all, are indispensable for special occasions.

Lighting bedrooms

Whether you are an night owl or a morning lark, the bedroom requires a sensitive combination of different types of lighting. The bedroom's principal function may be to provide restful surroundings for a peaceful night's sleep, but there is often the need to cater to a number of other activities as well, from reading, putting on makeup, or watching television to more intimate pleasures. An intensely personal place, the bedroom is also where we begin and end the day, transitional moments when we are acutely affected by the quality of light and general ambience.

Left: The tall, narrow shades of these unusual metal bedside lamps prevent the incandescent light source from being exposed and therefore avoid uncomfortable glare.

Below left: Adjustable lighting is essential for reading in bed.

Below: An awkwardly shaped alcove is cunningly mirrored to double the effect of an elegant bedside lamp.

Right: Sheer simplicity: an angled floor-standing lamp for reading in bed, tiny votive candles for atmosphere.

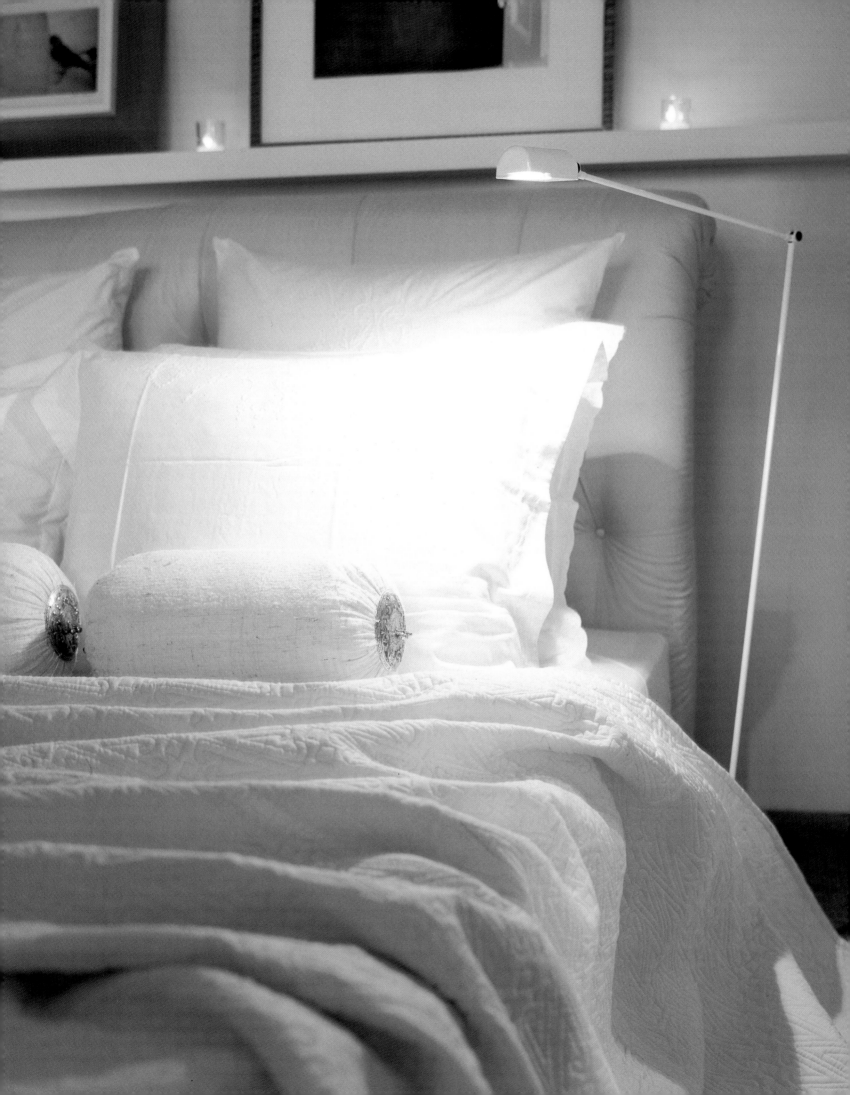

Most bedrooms today also serve as dressing areas, where makeup and clothing are put on, taken off, and stored. If you are lucky enough to have a large bedroom, and space is tight elsewhere in the home, you may even be tempted to include a working area for quiet study or paperwork. Where the bedroom is intended to serve more than one purpose, getting the lighting right is even more critical.

First of all, lighting must provide the right atmosphere for recharging the batteries. We spend much of our waking time in the bedroom in a state of tiredness after the day's activities. It is therefore important to avoid glare or extreme light conditions that would hurt weary eyes. Soft ambient light is not only important for relaxation, it is also vital if you like to watch television in bed.

Central or overhead fixtures are common arrangements in bedrooms, but these can provide a very unsympathetic quality of light. You will be lying down in bed for much of the time, and a central light will be more visible and intrusive. For general or ambient lighting, it is better to rely on wall lights behind the bed or table lamps beside it. Uplighting can also provide a good level

Left and above: The ultimate platform bed is artificially lit by a pair of floor-standing halogen spotlights, but the real drama is overhead. A curved double-glazed skylight, screened by pivoting aluminum louvers, can be opened hydraulically to reveal an unimpeded view of a dramatic city skyline.

Above and right: In the bedroom, as elsewhere in the house, the wide choice of light fixtures available makes it easy to choose a light that complements the overall decorative scheme.

of background light and generate a sense of warmth and security. General bedroom lighting should be dimmable; the right level for nighttime is unlikely to be adequate during the day.

Bedside light is critical. The last thing at night or the first thing on a dark morning, it is important to be able to switch a light on or off without getting out of bed. Small table lamps, task lights, and wall-mounted lights can all provide adequate light to read by in bed. The light should be positioned so it is high enough to illuminate the page and shaded in such a way that it does not

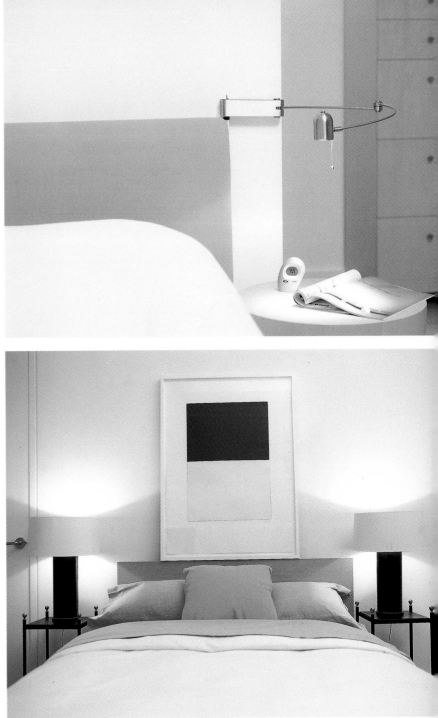

shine full in your face. You will need a light at both sides of a double bed, and each should be controlled separately for occasions when you want to read but your partner wants to sleep.

Fixtures with flexible, movable arms or supports that can be swiveled or angled, such as gooseneck wall lights, are particularly useful for bedtime reading. Reading in bed for long periods is not as comfortable as reading in a chair or at a desk, and you are likely to change position several times. A light that can be easily redirected is a bonus.

Sleeping and waking, undressing and dressing are closely related activities. But in terms of lighting, each has different requirements. You need to be able to see into closets or armoires to put clothes away or retrieve them, and mirrors and dressing areas need a good level of light for you to be able to assess your appearance. Dressing tables should be lit from both sides so that light falls evenly across your face. The same is true of wall mirrors. Light coming from above or below creates strong unattractive shadows, while backlighting, that seductive cinematic technique, may be exceptionally flattering but is hardly truthful. Avoid positioning lights in such a way that they shine directly onto a mirror, causing glare.

A pair of table lamps or wall lights, symmetrically positioned, can provide a welcome boost of illumination for a dressing table. Closets or built-in armoires can be lit by small bulbs that are triggered by the opening of the door.

As the baby becomes an inquisitive toddler, extra care should be taken for safety. Cover sockets that are not in use with blank plates or socket covers; keep hot light fixtures, cords, and switches out of reach. Freestanding lamps are easy for small children to knock down or pull over, so it is best to restrict lighting to mounted wall lights or ceiling lights that are well out of the way.

Many small children are afraid of the dark, but the soft glow of a nightlight will help to see them past this stage. Decorative lights in the shape of animals or figures are heavily marketed for this age group. Paper lanterns and fabric shades are also available in a wide variety of child-oriented designs.

Once your child is reading, the need for practical lighting increases. Robust task lights are good for the bedside; alternatively, a wall-mounted reading light over the head of the bed can be useful. School-age children have a increased need for task lighting. Desk lights are essential to encourage good study habits and prevent eyestrain. Computer work—and play—demands adequate levels of glare-free ambient light, together with more directional light targeted at the keyboard.

Right: Small halogen lights have been recessed into the wall of this child's bedroom, where they twinkle like stars in the night sky above a shipshaped bed with real ship's railings.

Above: Neon tubes, in alternating blue and pink, project over an extensive storage unit in a children's playroom.

Children's bedrooms have a different set of lighting demands. First and foremost, good lighting for children's rooms starts with a versatile infrastructure that can accommodate many changes of direction. Whatever age the child, it is important to make sure the lighting arrangements provide room for development. This may mean installing extra outlets for different layouts or increasing electrical needs in the future. Flexibility can also be served by installing free lighting track to power different fixtures in various positions, and by fitting dimmer switches.

In the early years, a baby may seem indifferent to the time of day or night, but you will require both a good level of ambient light for everyday routines as well as a softer light for nighttime feedings. A ceiling light, controlled by a dimmer, is good for general light, while plug-in nightlights or a small shaded lamp with a low-wattage bulb should provide adequate illumination in the small hours.

Right: Angled downlights, positioned to wash the walls with light, are a practical choice for children's rooms. In the early years, movable lamps can be a hazard.

Lighting bathrooms

Electricity and water are dangerous companions, and nowhere in the home do they come in closer proximity than in the bathroom. When planning lighting for the bathroom, it is essential to consult a qualified electrician (see page 187) in order to ensure that your proposals are safe and conform to official regulations.

Many bathrooms are on the small side, making it more difficult to maintain an appropriate distance between lights and wet areas. In family bathrooms, where children tend to splash about, the risks can multiply. Water is not only an efficient conductor of electricity—splashing a hot bulb can also cause it to shatter.

In general, freestanding, hanging, or adjustable light fixtures should be avoided, as well as standard sockets, switches, and cords. Recessed lights, sealed units where the metal parts of the fixture are not exposed, and fixtures that enclose the bulb completely all provide trouble-free bathroom lighting. Regulations regarding switches vary from country to country. In the United States, where switches are largely grounded, normal switches can be used inside the bathroom. In Britain, by contrast, bathroom lights must either be controlled by a pull cord inside the room or a switch outside the door.

Although these safety requirements impose certain limitations, there is no reason why bathroom lighting should be strictly utilitarian in either appearance or effect. There are many light

Above left: A pair of strip lights mounted vertically on each side of the mirror provides even, glare-free illumination.

Above center: A similar arrangement conceals a pair of fluorescent strip lights behind custom-designed baffles.

Above right: A low-voltage recessed downlight provides crisp, clean, and sparkling light. The glass brick partition makes the available light go further.

Left: Light fixtures that completely enclose the bulb, such as these recessed downlights, are ideal for bathroom use.

fixtures specifically designed for use in proximity with water, and some standard fixtures can also be used, provided there is no opportunity for water to come in contact with either the bulb or the electrical supply. There are also underwater fixtures that can be employed to great aesthetic impact.

Bathrooms used to be places that were low on atmosphere and comfort. All too often, the style and level of lighting did little to redress the situation, with a single bright overhead fixture being the norm in many households. Such an arrangement offers almost no visual delight; neither is it particularly functional. Bathrooms obviously require a certain amount of practical light to support activities such as shaving, washing, and putting on makeup, but they should also be lit creatively as well in order to serve the no less important needs for relaxation and retreat. Nowadays we go to a certain amount of trouble to make sure

bathing is an enjoyable and refreshing interlude—warm water, scented soaps, and thick towels are delightfully pampering to the senses. However, the whole experience can be severely undermined by harsh or unimaginative lighting.

Recessed downlights are both practical and appealing. Since the bathroom has many fixed features in its layout, downlighting can be installed without any fear that the arrangement will need to be altered in the future. A directional eyeball spot can be particularly useful if you like to read in the bath. Uplights or lights recessed in the walls are another good solution; the light reflected from the ceiling will provide soft background illumination without direct glare when you are lying in the bath relaxing. Unless you opt for waterproof fixtures, make sure wall lights are positioned well away from showers and are high enough not to be accidentally splashed.

Spectacular effects can be achieved by underwater lighting. Faucets and shower heads literally sparkle and glow when lit with fiber optics, while small waterproof lights installed in the base or sides of a bathtub will create memorable effects. Less exotic, hugely cheaper, but no less evocative are candles. Arranged around the side of the bathtub, on glass shelving, or floating on the water, candles transform bathing into the ultimate sybaritic experience. The small twinkling points, multiplied in the reflections on glass bottles, shelves, and mirror, are charming and magical.

On the practical side, good functional lighting is required for the area around the sink and mirror. It is important to strike a balance between harsh truth and outright flattery. Bright and revealing light, combined with a mirror, may be just a little too uncompromising, especially first thing in the morning. On the other hand, too moody a light does not tell the whole story and is useless for judging the finer points of the appearance.

Above left and center: Tiny recessed halogen downlights cast a twinkly white light that is ideally suited to sleek glass, chrome, and marble bathroom fixtures. Here, they are positioned strategically over a tub and basin, while a dimmable wall light with a frosted glass shade provides more atmospheric light levels beside the tub (on the left).

Above: A slim chrome picture light mounted above a mirror adds a touch of plush theatricality to a small, richly decorated washroom. In general, however, toplighting a mirror is not the most flattering or informative arrangement, as it tends to throw the lower parts of the face into heavy shadow.

Again, a single overhead light, either above the mirror or mounted on the ceiling, is an inflexible and ineffective solution. Heavy toplighting of this kind creates hard shadows on the face that are unflattering and uninformative. The answer is to light the face as evenly as possible from the top and from each side. This can be achieved in several ways: lights can be recessed in the ceiling and walls to illuminate the mirror on three sides; a pair of tubes or wall lights can be used to flank the mirror; or you may wish to adopt the more conspicuous glamour of mounting a series of globe

Aside from the area around the sink, bathroom lighting need not be very strong. High levels of bright lighting in the bathroom are a hangover from the days when this room was treated as a strictly functional space and furnished accordingly. Lower ambient light levels are much more conducive to relaxation and are less likely to cause incidental glare by reflecting off hard tiled or shiny surfaces, such as porcelain appliances, mirrors, and glass. For maximum flexibility of mood and ambience, install a dimmer switch on the main bathroom lights.

As far as light sources are concerned, incandescent is warming, soothing, flattering, and more compatible with period-style decoration, while halogen is crisper, cooler, ideally suited to contemporary styles of decoration, and more accurate as far as color relationships go. It is also important to maximize the effect of natural light in the bathroom, the most truthful and potentially beautiful light source of all. Frosted, etched, or colored window glass will all diffuse and pattern the light in intriguing ways without compromising privacy, but surely the most dramatic of all must be pure light falling from a skylight that has been strategically placed over the bathtub.

lamps around its perimeter. If you intend to use multiple lights, remember that each lamp can be of a relatively low wattage, such as 25 watts, since you will be using many of them.

Information light may also be needed. Some bathroom mirrors are illuminated, and mirrored cabinets are also available with their own integral light for shaving. A small light inside the cabinet itself and triggered by the opening of the door can also be useful for reading the labels of cosmetics or medicines.

Above left: An adjustable period-style wall light creates soft and rich ambient illumination.

Above center: A pair of wall lights are mounted over double glass basins. The wall itself is covered with sheets of acid-etched glass with integral mirrored circles.

Above right: Three-part wall sconces in frosted glass and polished chrome have a retro appeal.

Lighting workrooms

Aside from the general routine of household activities, many homes today include areas devoted to concentrated work of various kinds. The area in question may be anything from a corner of a living room to a basement workshop or a fully equipped home office. Whether you are running a business or simply tinkering with a favorite project, proper lighting will increase your productivity and enjoyment.

Working from home is a definite demographical trend. If you are setting up your main or supplementary work space at home, you must pay careful attention to the lighting; it is not enough simply to go along with existing arrangements. Regulations govern the installation of commercial lighting to minimize employees' eye-strain; but in large businesses, economic factors also come into play. The unfortunate result in many office buildings is a relatively poor quality of light, with flickering from fluorescent sources and glare from inappropriately positioned fixtures being the most

Below: A working area is neatly slotted in under a mezzanine, positioned to gain benefit from the natural light from above. Two wall lights on adjustable arms serve as task lighting.

Above: A decorative table lamp makes an elegant addition to an ornate desk in a Milan apartment.

common causes of complaint. At home, there is no need and every reason not to duplicate such uncomfortable conditions. On the other hand, all close work must be supplemented by effective task lighting: concentrating on aesthetics may provide a pleasant environment, but not a very efficient one.

Task lighting is essential for the desk. If you are using a computer, task light should be angled to fall on the keyboard, not the screen; if you are writing or drawing, the light should fall on the page or sheet without shining in your eyes. There are many excellent task lights on the market that provide adjustable, directional light with little side spill. Position the task light so it illuminates your work from the side and so the light source itself is hidden from view. Lights that have long adjustable arms are particularly useful, as you can vary the height to change the spread of light from a tight, close focus to a more diffuse desktop level of illumination. Task light is first and foremost practical light, but it serves an important psychological purpose as well. Sitting in a bright pool of light seems to concentrate the mind and helps shut out distractions—a valuable asset if you are working in a room that is generally used for other activities.

is not only uplifting, it is also excellent to work by. The solution is to use venetian blinds, translucent curtains, or blinds that either pull up or pull down to half-shield the light.

For work that requires fine color judgments, a north-lit work space is ideal. If you have no such suitable location in your home, daylight simulation lamps are useful. These are colored blue and come in a wide variety of formats for different fixtures. Alternatively, halogen makes a good all-purpose light source for working areas.

Utility areas, such as laundry rooms, workshops, and garages are ideal locations for the economical and practical light provided by fluorescent tubes. Mounted on the ceiling, tube lights will cast an evenly diffused bright illumination over the whole area that is adequate to work by in most situations. If your activities in such areas involve potentially hazardous equipment, such as machinery or sharp tools, you will need additional task lighting over the work area. Remember that moving equipment in combination with fluorescent light can create a strobe effect, so if you intend to use moving machinery, choose high-frequency fluorescent or tungsten-halogen lighting. As in the kitchen, the task light should be focused on the surface in front of you and its source concealed from view to avoid shadows and glare. A strip light mounted on the wall or under a shelf behind a baffle provides a no-nonsense solution.

Above: The clean lines of this modern work area are enhanced by a contemporary lighting classic, the "Tolomeo," by Michele de Lucchi and Giancarlo Fassina. It features a handle at the base of the shade for easy repositioning.

Right: An adjustable desk light provides targeted illumination for a computer keyboard. Light must be always be directed so it is not reflected on the screen.

Task light alone is not enough: the contrast between bright task light and dim surroundings can be tiring. In work areas, ambient light is often best provided by uplighting the ceiling to create a gentle overhead level of illumination without shadows or glare. Uplighting is also highly recommended for computer work, since there is no risk of reflections obscuring the visibility of the screen. In the more relaxed surroundings of a traditional study, ambient lighting can be provided by a series of table or floor lamps.

Working from home also entails managing natural light levels. Direct sunlight can interfere with the computer screen in the same way it can make a television hard to see. The answer is to angle the screen away from the window and reduce the strength of the natural light by partially screening the window. It is important, however, not to block out all daylight; natural light

Lighting outdoors

Exterior lighting adds an extra dimension to both home and yard. Apart from information or security light for illuminating paths and entrances, most outdoor lighting is essentially decorative, accentuating the finer points of architecture or planting. In many people's minds, exterior lighting is associated with majestically floodlit monuments and *Dynasty*-style estates. But you don't need to live in a palatial home set in acres of ground to exploit its potential. If you enjoy your yard by day, outdoor lighting will extend the pleasure after dark and enhance outdoor living areas for eating, relaxing, and entertaining.

Exterior lighting needs its own servicing infrastructure, and it is important to consult a qualified professional to plan and carry out the installation for you. Safety is a prime consideration. Constant exposure to weather and extremes of temperature (and in seaside areas to salt corrosion) place high demands on both fixtures and cables, and there are stringent regulations in force governing the equipment that can be used and its positioning. Outdoor fixtures should be kept clear of leaves and debris, and cables must be buried or routed so there is no risk of contact with lawn mowers or other garden tools. Switching should be arranged so that lights are fully controllable from indoors, and an earthed leakage trip should be incorporated into the circuit.

Broadly speaking, there are two main types of external power supply: standard household-current and low voltage. Each has its own advantages and disadvantages; systems that combine both types of supply are also possible. For a more detailed account, see Household electrical supplies, pages 178–179.

Another important practical consideration is the question of light pollution. Bright exterior light contributes to the spill of illumination that emanates from many of our urban and suburban areas, canceling out the evocative sight of starry nights and, more critically, wasting energy and disrupting the natural biorhythms of wild creatures. On a more local level, overlighting is unneighborly. A high level of exterior illumination can cause unwelcome glare to shine through the windows of adjacent houses.

Exterior lighting does not need to be bright to be effective. In fact, the most imaginative outdoor schemes are based on no more than small, focused accents of light. The object of the exercise is to create a sense of magic and delight that both transforms the backyard and tempts you to carry on enjoying it after the sun goes down.

Right: An industrial-style exterior light mounted on a side wall supplements light spilling from the interior on a roof terrace.

Lighting entrances

Entrance lighting is the most common form of exterior illumination, not least because of its obvious practical advantages. Lighting front doors, porches, steps, paths, driveways, and garage entrances helps you and your visitors negotiate the way safely at night and is a proven deterrent for prowlers. And entrance lighting has aesthetic benefits, too. A well-lit approach is warm and hospitable and adds psychological comfort to homecoming.

If you live in a row house in a built-up area that is well served by street lighting, you may only need to light the front door, house number, bell or knocker, and keyhole. But if your home is separated out or more remotely situated, you may need a series of lights at key points along the main entranceway, together with lights strategically placed around the building.

When lighting any exterior entrance—front door, side door, or garage—a number of practical issues have to be addressed. The light level should be high enough to be informative, and lights should be positioned at key points to guide the route. At the same time, however, light sources should be diffused or concealed to prevent glare, which can be equally dangerous for motorists and pedestrians alike. There are also the issues of economy and energy conservation. Lights burning all night are expensive and wasteful. One solution is to install long-lasting and low-energy compact fluorescents in outdoor fixtures; the other is to put the lights on switches that are triggered by movement or heat. In addition to such "approach" lighting, there is also a form of switching that is light-detecting, responding when natural light levels fall or rise, but this does result in lights burning all night. For more complex installations, covering a larger area of ground, it is often a good idea to consult a security firm that can devise an anti-intruder system. Approach lighting is best run on a separate circuit from decorative exterior lighting.

Front door lighting must be visually appealing as well as practical. Carriage lamps and lanterns dominate the market, but it is worth exploring less expected solutions. In any case, the carriage lamp, with its rather grand Victorian overtones, can look incongruous if your house lacks such period or architectural credentials. Simple omnidirectional globes are elegant and versatile; bulkhead fixtures are practical and vandalproof. Lit glass panels

Above: A pair of Venetian-inspired wall sconces with pagoda tops provide both informative and atmospheric light at each side of a handsome doorway.

Above: Sandblasted glass diffuses interior light but preserves nighttime privacy, creating a glowing panel that accentuates the careful geometry of the architectural planes.

Left: Concealed sources are just as important outside as in. Here, the building is subtly lit by a hidden uplight; other uplights hidden among the foliage add atmosphere.

illuminating the house number make stylish information lights. Pairs of lights are generally better for even, shadow-free illumination than a single source on one side of the door.

Paths, driveways, steps, and gates also need to be well lit. Approach lighting is advantageous in this context, too. To avoid glare, lights should be positioned at a low level and diffused. Spiked spotlights can be angled to pick out a path or focused where light is needed; lanterns or mock streetlights are less appropriate and overly reminiscent of a municipal park. Alternatively, decorative outdoor lighting may generate enough light on its own to illuminate the entrance to your home.

Lighting buildings

If your home has great architectural character, lighting the exterior of the building can bring its best features to the fore. "Floodlighting" is the common term for architectural lighting, but it tends to give people the wrong idea of the purpose of such illumination. The object of the exercise should not be to wash the outside of the house with a bright, even light, but to highlight textures and details in a understated, intriguing way.

Floodlighting in its proper sense is a subtle as a sledgehammer. Football stadia—and prisons—are floodlit for good practical reasons. Unfortunately, so too are many public buildings and monuments, much to the detriment of our cityscapes. Good exterior lighting works with architectural details, enhancing features, adding textural interest, and emphasizing the modeling of facades. Bad exterior lighting flattens out contrasts, penetrates the interior with glare, and spills out into the wider context of the building's setting. In the public realm, the choice of economical sources of light, such as high- and low-pressure sodium, makes matters worse. The orange cast and poor color rendering of these types of light can reduce the richest combination of materials and surface treatments to the lowest common visual denominator.

Unless your house is very grand, effective exterior lighting can be achieved very simply with several low-level lights, carefully positioned so they graze the facade obliquely. Spotlights and other lights with a fairly close focus are preferable to fixtures that create a broader wash or beam, which might spill well beyond the boundaries of your own property.

Left: Halogen exterior-rated uplights recessed in the ground throw the surface of a perimeter wall into relief and cast evocative reflections on the surface of the pool.

Lighting the yard

Devising a lighting plan for the yard is more akin to painting with light than using light as a practical tool. Aesthetic effect is all important, which means thinking carefully about color, level, and positioning for maximum impact.

Color is a key aspect. The French have an evocative term for twilight: *l'heure bleue*, which beautifully describes the time of day when the sky and landscape share the same cool tone. After the sun sets, our eyes become slightly more sensitive to the bluer end of the spectrum; moonlight and starlight are also silvery in color. While the most "natural" yard lighting would emphasize this bluish cast, psychologically we are drawn to warm pools of light when it comes to relaxing, eating, and enjoying the company of friends. Garden lighting therefore needs to provide a mixture of cool and warm sources—cool for highlighting areas of planting and warm for outdoor living areas. This mixture can be achieved by combining incandescent and candles with halogen sources.

As far as light levels are concerned, resist the attempt to turn night into day. Keep individual sources dim to avoid light pollution and glare. The overall light level outdoors at night will always be low, so there is a risk of uncomfortable contrast between any light and its surroundings. Where supplementary light is required, near cooking or eating areas, for example, cluster temporary lights such as candles together to give an extra boost of illumination.

Exterior lighting will have an impact on internal rooms and views. If the light is too bright outdoors, it will skew the balance unfavorably; conversely, exterior lighting can be boosted by "borrowed" light shining through windows and glass doors. "Halfway" rooms like conservatories, which are wholly or partially glazed, provide good vantage points for admiring exterior lighting. However, if the light indoors is too bright, the expanse of glass will act as a mirror, rendering the views invisible. Downlights or uplights positioned at low levels both inside and outside, with the sources concealed, will preserve the transparency of the glazing. It may take some experimenting to get the levels right.

Outdoors, sources should be concealed if possible and positioned at a low level. A number of small points of accent light, carefully positioned to emphasize outdoor features, will lend great vitality and atmosphere. Treat the yard as a series of interconnecting spaces rather than a single area that needs to be uniformly lit.

Left: A waterproof spotlight turns a garden pool into a mysterious nighttime grotto, the magical effect enhanced by an array of tiny, sparkling votive candles.

tree reveals a graphic silhouette, which can be very effective, especially for the bare branches of deciduous trees in winter. Frontal lighting reveals foliage more clearly, but may leave the upper part of the tree in darkness. Direct uplighting can create a highly dramatic effect, making leaves and branches glisten in the light. Other outdoor features, such as pots, urns, and ornaments, can be lit in exactly the same way that you would light a decorative object indoors, using low-level lights, positioned to one side of the feature to accentuate form, from behind to silhouette shape, or spotlighting from above for drama.

Pools, ponds, and fountains provide the perfect excuse for striking outdoor lighting effects. A sheet of water is a reflective surface; at night, carefully judged lighting adds to the mirror effect. Lighting the perimeter of a pool or pond or lighting plants set alongside it is theatrical and romantic. Waterproof fixtures can also be sunk in the water to create a glowing focal point. Special waterproof fixtures are available for use under or in close proximity to water.

Paths and outdoor seating areas need to be adequately lit for safety and practicality, but this does not necessarily mean you have to compromise on atmosphere. A common outdoor lighting mistake is to illuminate paths and terraces too brightly, throwing

Above: Votives, essentially simple candles in protective metal casings, provide an instant and economical way of creating magical effects with outdoor lighting.

Right: Candles in decorative pierced lanterns create intriguing patterns of light and shade. Concealed spotlights pick out the simple water feature.

Almost any garden feature will benefit from sensitive lighting. A specimen tree, a wall covered in ivy, a pool or fountain can all be transformed into magical focal points at night. Use light to emphasize contrasts in texture and to cast interesting patterns of shadow. Backlit foliage, the silhouetted forms of garden structures, spotlit ornaments and urns all provide a compellingly theatrical dimension. You can also play tricks with scale and proportion. A series of lanterns, receding into the distance, will make a garden seem bigger and more mysterious than it really is.

Garden plantings, from small shrubs to full-size trees, look best illuminated from a low level, either with small spotlights angled upward, uplights sunk in the ground, or low-level downlights. Spiked or half-buried uplights tucked away within a border create dramatic light for foliage, throwing leaf shapes into relief. Plants that are denser, such as trees and large shrubs, may require more than one light to define their full size and shape. Backlighting a

Above: The atmospheric glow of these hanging lanterns provides just enough illumination for eating outside.

Above right: Tiny dancing points of candlelight delicately pick out an exterior stairway.

Right: Outdoor lighting should be subtle and evocative. The object is not to provide a substitute for daylight but to accent surfaces and textures.

more interesting surfaces and planted areas into relative darkness. Instead of bright downlighting, an outdoor stairway or path can be picked out using a series of low-level diffused lights positioned along its length. Similarly, low-level downlights or uplights around the perimeter of a paved area can provide enough illumination to be informative without flooding the entire area with light.

If you intend to cook and eat outside frequently, you will need a higher level of light around the barbeque and the table. Position lights in front and on each side of the cooking area to avoid working in your shadow. Tables can be downlit by spotlights mounted overhead, on a framework of trellising, for example. Candles are the ideal accompaniment to outdoor entertaining. Citronella candles double as insect repellents, while spiked garden flares add a touch of grandeur.

Practicalities

Light and color

The subject of intense scientific inquiry for centuries, light is a peculiar phenomenon. A form of electromagnetic radiation with unique properties and characteristics, it has a curious dual nature, behaving both as a particle and a wave of energy. As a wave, light travels from a light source in radiating straight lines until it hits an obstacle in its path. As a particle, units of light have no mass, but exist only in motion.

Natural light, the light from the sun that makes our world visible, is the point of comparison for all artificial alternatives. We deem natural light to be "white," a blend of all the colors in the spectrum. This can be demonstrated by the familiar experiment of breaking up a beam of sunlight with a prism to reveal the spectrum colors of red, orange, yellow, green, blue, indigo, and violet. All of these colors mixed or blended in equal parts make white light.

Each different part of the spectrum has its own wavelength, measured in nanometers, or millionths of a millimeter. Our eyes are only sensitive enough to pick up the portion of the spectrum equivalent to a range of between 400 and 700 nanometers. The invisible part of the electromagnetic spectrum extends below 400 nanometers to the shorter ultraviolet rays, x-rays, and gamma rays and above 700 nanometers to the longer wavelengths of infrared.

Artificial light sources can only approximate the balanced effect of bright natural daylight. Some are close replicas of white light, while others are much more obviously tinted. This has important implications for the way we perceive colors.

Contrary to popular belief, color is not an inherent characteristic of an object. A red apple is not red in itself, rather it absorbs all the wavelengths of light except the red, which it reflects back to our eyes. In conditions of white light, where the colors are balanced across the spectrum, colors will be "true." But where the light itself is skewed to a certain part of the spectrum, our perception of color relationships will necessarily be affected.

measurements shown in degrees Kelvin

8,000

7,500

7,000

Northern blue sky
Light from the northern sky has a cool blue tone and a rating of 8,000 degrees Kelvin and above.

6,500

6,000

5,500

Direct sunlight at midday
Natural midday sunlight is the whitest light of all, measuring approximately 5,500 degrees Kelvin.

5,000

4,500

4,000

Halogen bulb
Halogen light is appreciably cooler than that of incandescent, with a color temperature of more than 3,000 degrees Kelvin.

3,500

3,000

150-watt incandescent bulb
Incandescent bulbs emit most of their light in the yellow to red end of the spectrum and have a low color temperature of 2,900 degrees Kelvin.

2,500

2,000

Candle
The soft yellow glow of candlelight, at around 2,000 degrees Kelvin, is the warmest light source of all.

1,500

1,000

Overcast sky
An overcast sky casts
a cool bluish light that
measures between 6,500-
7,500 degrees Kelvin.

Fluorescent bulbs
Visually, fluorescent light
is cool and bright, rated at
up to 5,000 degrees Kelvin,
but in recent years bulb
manufacturers have
developed new types of
fluorescent that cast a
warmer light, measured at
between 2,500 and 3,000
degrees Kelvin.

Color temperature

The tone of light is defined as its "color
temperature," or how the light looks in terms
of white. It is measured in degrees Kelvin.
Paradoxically, the higher the color temperature,
the cooler the effect of the light. The color
temperature of a particular type of light depends
on its wavelength pattern (see page 171). For
example, if you were to refract light from an
ordinary incandescent bulb through a prism,
the colors split by the prism would not be evenly
balanced, as they are for white light, but would
fall mainly in the red and yellow portion of the
spectrum. Measured as color temperature, this
would give a reading of about 2,900 degrees
Kelvin. To our eyes, this light looks warm, cast
with the mellow tones of red and yellow.
Candlelight, at 2,000 degrees Kelvin, is warmer
still, while an overcast sky, measured at around
7,500 degrees Kelvin, is cool and bluish. Natural
midday sunlight falls around the middle of the
visible spectrum, at 5,500 degrees Kelvin.

40-watt incandescent bulb
With most of its light
in the yellow to red end
of the spectrum, a low-wattage
incandescent bulb casts a
warm light that, at 2,500
degrees Kelvin, is only slightly
cooler than candlelight.

Color rendering

While color temperature affects the appearance of the light source itself, color rendering has to do with the way the light affects the color of the objects it illuminates. The effect of light on color is dependent on the spectral wavelength of the light source. Cool fluorescent light, for example, has a color temperature that closely approximates daylight, but when we view its spectral pattern it is immediately apparent that it has spectral peaks of green and orange, which can distort the appearance of colors in an unacceptable way.

There are variations, too, in the way our eyes respond to different wavelengths of light. During the day we see most effectively within the middle of the spectrum—the range from green to yellow—which is why a green landscape is so soothing and restful, and why green blinds, green shades, and green glass were traditionally considered to be good for the eyes. At night, this range shifts slightly toward blue—think of how gray, white, and blue flowers can suddenly appear so luminous at twilight.

For these reasons, it is difficult to quantify the color rendering characteristics of different light sources, since so much depends on the context in which they will be used. Comparing photographs of the same interior lit by different light sources can be a useful guide to assessing visual difference but, in the end, it all boils down to what looks and feels right.

Energy efficiency and lifespan

Other factors that may be more readily defined are the energy efficiency of the light source and, related to this, its lifespan. In general, the more balanced a light source is across the color spectrum—in other words, the better it is at rendering colors faithfully—the more energy it consumes to produce that light. Among the most energy-efficient and economical of all light sources is low-pressure sodium, which is in common use as streetlighting. The light emitted by these lamps is concentrated in the central or yellow part of the spectrum, the portion to which our eyes respond most sensitively. Not only are such

lights very economical to run, but also the level of light need not be so high for our eyes to make sense of the world. In terms of providing adequate illumination after dark, low-pressure sodium is informative and highly cost-effective. But the price of such characteristics is almost total loss of color differentiation.

The more energy-efficient light sources, such as fluorescent, tend to have longer lifespans. But lifespan can also be affected by the way a lamp is used. For example, frequently switching an incandescent lamp off and on will shorten its life dramatically. Lifespan itself can be a relative measure. Incandescent lamps function at full capacity until they burn out, while fluorescent lamps gradually fade away in a continuous decline of light level. Dimmers can extend the lifespan of some lamps significantly.

Opposite: These simplified diagrams of the spectral wavelengths of different light sources graphically demonstrate their different color rendering properties.

Below: Fluorescent light has spikes in the yellow and green part of the spectrum, and therefore highlights cool yellow tones.

Below: Incandescent light sources, with their heavy weighting toward the red part of the spectrum, cast a warm mellow light.

Below: As halogen has a well-balanced spectral pattern close to that of daylight, its color fidelity is extremely good.

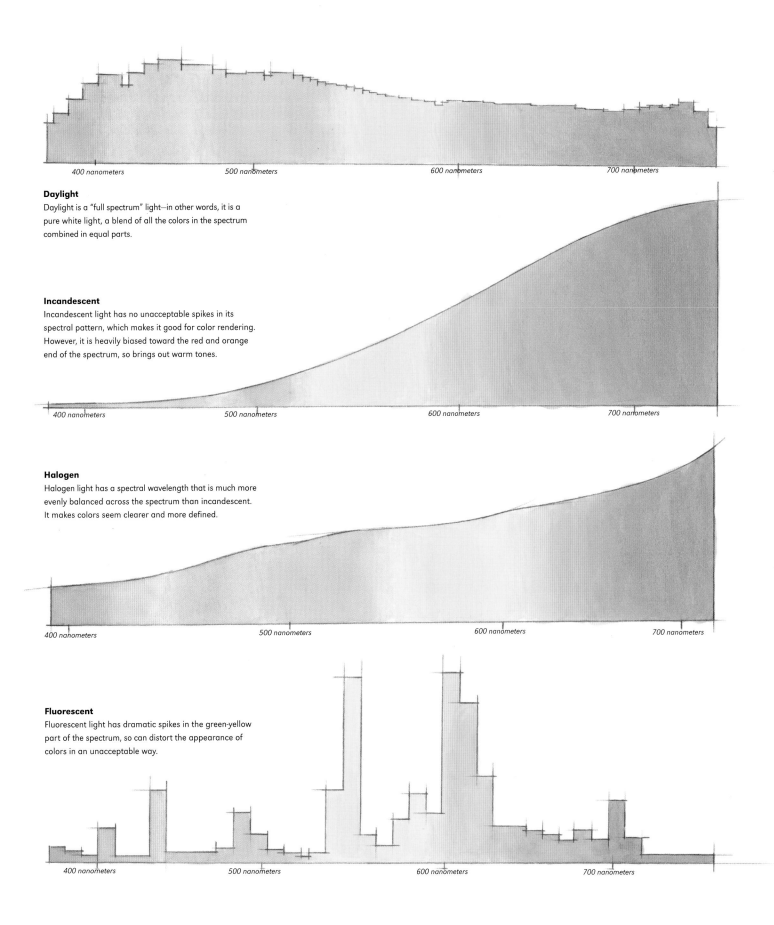

400 nanometers   *500 nanometers*   *600 nanometers*   *700 nanometers*

Daylight
Daylight is a "full spectrum" light—in other words, it is a pure white light, a blend of all the colors in the spectrum combined in equal parts.

400 nanometers   *500 nanometers*   *600 nanometers*   *700 nanometers*

Incandescent
Incandescent light has no unacceptable spikes in its spectral pattern, which makes it good for color rendering. However, it is heavily biased toward the red and orange end of the spectrum, so brings out warm tones.

400 nanometers   *500 nanometers*   *600 nanometers*   *700 nanometers*

Halogen
Halogen light has a spectral wavelength that is much more evenly balanced across the spectrum than incandescent. It makes colors seem clearer and more defined.

400 nanometers   *500 nanometers*   *600 nanometers*   *700 nanometers*

Fluorescent
Fluorescent light has dramatic spikes in the green-yellow part of the spectrum, so can distort the appearance of colors in an unacceptable way.

Analyzing your needs

Lighting is inescapably bound up with function, with tasks and activities. The first step in the process of designing a lighting scheme is to analyze your requirements. How much light do you need? Where should lights go? Which lights should be fixed and which lights should be flexible?

Professional lighting designers have to combine aesthetic flair with considerable technical expertise. Faced with the challenge of designing a new lighting scheme for a gymnasium, theater, museum, shopping mall or hotel foyer, gut instinct is not enough. Such environments may have no real precedent in terms of design and layout or they may present very specific lighting requirements arising out of the different activities that they accommodate. It is essential, therefore, that lighting designers should be able to calculate with some degree of precision how much light a space will require. They do this by means of somewhat complex calculations that measure how much light flows from a given source,

how much light actually arrives at a surface, and how much light is then reflected back. In technical terms, the flow of light from a light source is measured in "lumens"; the amount of light that arrives at a surface is measured in "lux," or foot candles; and the luminance of a surface, or the amount of light that is reflected off it, is measured in "candelas." By consulting recommended lux levels for specific tasks, requirements, or types of interior, designers can then work out exactly how to deliver the amount of light required.

Below: The walls, ceiling, and floor of a room reflect different amounts of the light that falls on them, depending on their color and finish. The amount of light reflected from a surface is known as its reflectance and it is measured as a percentage. A white surface reflects 80 percent of the light that strikes it, and therefore a room with white walls and ceiling will provide a bright, even level of light.

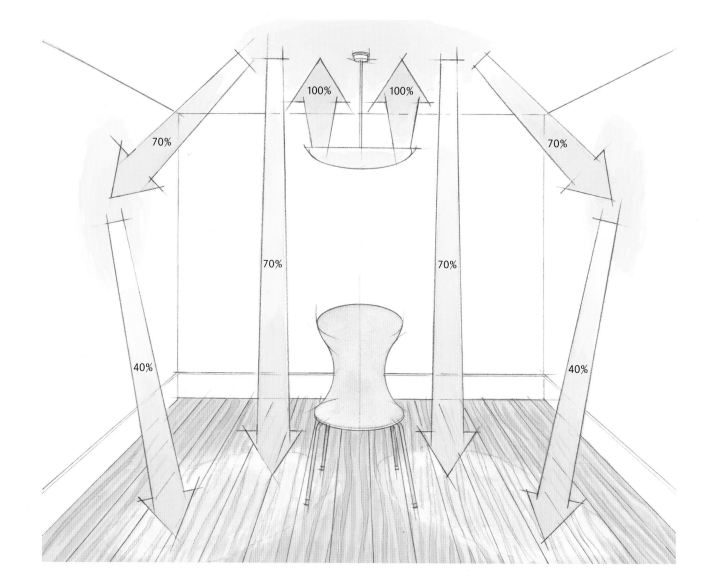

All this is fairly meaningless for the home lighting designer. Talk of the "flow of light" only generates confusion: the majority of us have a technical grasp of the subject on a par with the eccentric aunt in a James Thurber story, who imagined electrical current leaking from her sockets like water from a tap. But what such measurements illustrate, although we may have neither the equipment nor the need to take them, is that the amount of light in an interior is not purely determined by the brightness of a lamp, but is also affected by the direction of the light, the distance of the lamp from a surface, and the quality of the surface itself. In lighting terms, the amount of light reflected off a surface is known as reflectance, and it is measured as a percentage.

Light-colored surfaces, such as white-painted brick, white plaster, or pale marble will absorb 30 percent of the light that hits them, reflecting between 60 and 80 percent; while walls and floors that are painted a dark color, will absorb 85–95 percent of the light that hits them, reflecting only 10–15 percent, even as little as 5 percent, if the surface is matte and black. The room may be the same, and the same wattage lamp may be used, but differences in surface will radically affect the general light level. It is important to bear these measurements in mind when planning interior decoration. A room with a white ceiling and walls will provide an excellent distribution of light; a room with a white ceiling and dark walls will create adequate distribution; and a room with dark ceiling and walls has very low reflectance and therefore the light levels too will be low. An interior with a dark ceiling and walls will require many more light sources and higher wattage bulbs to achieve a light level as high as that in a room with light-colored walls.

As mentioned above, texture is another important factor. Matte finishes, such as plaster, brickwork, and fabric, absorb and diffuse light while glossy, shiny surfaces, such as glass and marble, reflect it. Since light is absorbed by each surface it bounces off, the light direction will also make a difference. Highly directional light, such as fixed downlights or an angled desk lamp, for example, focuses a high level of illumination onto a relatively small area. This area will be brighter the closer it is to the light source, but immediately outside the beam light levels will be low. More ambient lighting, which may bounce off the ceiling then reflect from the walls, will result in a lower light level, as each of these surfaces will have absorbed some of the light.

In practice, it is simply not necessary to measure light levels in the home. Domestic space is not as diverse as public or commercial space, and you can usually rely on experience, common sense, and what feels right when judging whether light levels are adequate. Nevertheless, a few figures may provide some useful and informative points of comparison. Fifty lux is the minimum required to see and move safely in a space but provides little perception of color or detail (some valuable paintings and textiles that may suffer from light damage need to be kept in conditions where the light levels are below 50 lux). The correct level for a dimmed theater auditorium is 100 lux, while 200 lux is a comfortable level for rooms where no concentrated work is carried out. When assessing how much light a room will need, it is essential to consider the tasks and activities that will take place in that space—a room where close work such as sewing takes place will require higher light levels than a room that is devoted entirely to watching television. General workrooms, such as kitchens, where some detail and color differentiation is required, demand a level of approximately 300–500 lux. Reading and clerical work need a level of 500–750 lux, but work requiring intense concentration on fine print or small components or requiring subtle color differentiation needs a level of 1,000 lux or more. Natural daylight is dazzling in comparison: the light level outdoors when the sky is overcast is 5,000 lux, and on a clear, sunny day, lux levels can rise to 100,000 lux.

It is also worth bearing in mind that the amount of light we need increases with age. At the age of forty, we require three times more light to perform tasks than a ten-year-old; while by the age of sixty, we require a staggering fifteen times as much.

Obviously, such guidelines are only approximate. Lighting, after all, is a matter of taste as much as technicality. What may be comfortable for one person may be sepulchral to another and dazzling to a third. The best way to assess whether you've got it right is to experiment. For a modest outlay, you can buy a number of inexpensive lights to try out different light directions and positions. Directional lights, such as clip-on spots, are useful for assessing the impact of uplighting, downlighting, or angled light, while small portable table lamps provide a guide to the effect of ambient lighting. Using extension cords, and with the help of a friend if necessary, try out several different locations and combinations. It is also a good idea to furnish yourself with a range of bulbs of various wattages to assess the impact of different sources and light levels.

You can try out your ideas or analyze an existing lighting scheme using a camera. Take several photographs of the room you want to light from as wide a viewpoint as possible and without using a flash. Because film is not as sensitive as the human eye and lacks the eye's inherent tendency to correct discrepancies in light levels, your photographs will reveal the current lighting conditions in an exaggerated form and will show you exactly where more depth and focus is needed.

Once you have established where you need more light, the next step is to to consult a qualified electrician (see page 187) to discover how best to achieve the results you want. He or she will be able to assess your lighting infrastructure and let you know if your options are limited by a dated electrical installation. However, before turning to the professionals, it is worth making a sketch plan of the room you intend to light; this will play an important role in analyzing your needs and help you decide where to place light fittings, what kinds to use, and where to position new outlets and switches (see pages 174–175). Armed with this invaluable information, you will be able to plan an effective and successful lighting scheme that meets all of your requirements.

Making a sketch plan

Measure the room you intend to light and make a scale drawing on graph paper. Mark all the existing architectural features, including fireplaces, alcoves, windows, doors, and large pieces of furniture. Note the position of existing electrical outlets, switches, and central moldings. The two plans shown are marked with questions that will help you think about the type of activities and features your lighting scheme must accommodate, make the most of the natural light in the room, and also identify any problem areas.

How much natural light does the room receive?
Window treatments have a direct effect on the amount of natural light in an interior. Shades and drapes that pull back from the window allow as much light as possible to penetrate the room.

Key

⊠ **Outlet**
⊗ **Central molding**
▣ **Switch**

Is an area of the room required for concentrated work?
If so, you will need a good task light to illuminate the worksurface.

Are there any dark corners?
If so, make sure there is an outlet in the area, which will allow you to add a versatile clip-on spot or even a table or floor lamp.

Is there a central ceiling light?
The central ceiling light is one of the most common light fixtures, but it is not necessarily the most effective solution to lighting a room. Consider other fixtures, such as track lighting, which powers a number of individual lights for a more flexible lighting scheme.

Does the switch by the door activate only the ceiling light?
A "dual outlet" system will allow you to control individual lights both at the door and at the fixture itself.

Are there enough outlets in the room?
Increasing the number of outlets is an obvious way of providing flexibility, since it allows changes to be made to lighting and furniture arrangements in the future. Freestanding lamps such as floor lamps also add flexibility to a lighting scheme, as they are easily moved.

Are there special features or items you wish to highlight?
A picture light will illuminate paintings but it will not allow you to move them at a later date, as the light is fixed to the wall.

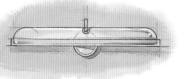

Which direction does the window face?
The orientation of the room will affect the light in the interior. North light is cooler and whiter than the light cast from the south. If possible, be flexible about the layout of your home. Choose sunnier rooms for living spaces, and darker rooms for bedrooms, as they are mostly used after dark and thus largely seen in artificial light.

Do existing light fixtures cause glare?
Central or overhead light fixtures can provide an unsympathetic quality of light or even cause glare. This is especially true in the bedroom, where you will be lying in bed for much of the time. If you wish to have an overhead light, choose a fixture that screens the light source.

Are the existing lights dimmable?
In most rooms, apart from workrooms, lighting should be dimmable—the gentle level of light suitable for nighttime will not be adequate during the day.

Is there more than one entrance/exit?
If so, there should be switches at both entrance and exit points. In a bedroom, the main light should also be controllable from the bedside, allowing you to turn it off without getting out of bed.

Does the lighting allow for all the activities that will take place in the room?
In a bedroom, bedside light is essential. You will need a light at either side of a double bed and each one should be controlled separately, allowing you to read while your partner sleeps, or vice versa.

What activities will take place in the room?
In a bedroom, dressing and putting on makeup are two likely activities. Dressing tables need a good level of light. They should be lit from each side to create an even fall of light.

Are there built-in features, such as closets, which need lighting?
Dark closets can be illuminated by small bulbs triggered by the opening of the door, allowing you to put clothes away and retrieve them with ease.

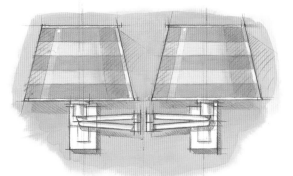

Bulbs

A bewildering range of light bulbs, or lamps as they are correctly known, is available today. This section profiles a selection of the most widely used bulbs on the market and briefly explains the form and function of each one. Different types of bulb have strong associations with particular types of light source. For more information on how each light source functions, its characteristics, energy efficiency, lifespan, and other advantages and disadvantages, turn to pages 48–67. For details of how different light sources affect color, turn to pages 168–171.

Incandescent lamps

Incandescent lamps have been in use for nearly a century (the first incandescent bulbs had a carbon filament, but this was replaced by a tungsten filament in 1907) and they are still the most familiar and widely used lamps. Incandescent lamps require no additional equipment, as they can be run directly from the household current. They are available in a number of different shapes and sizes.

1 Standard GLS frosted
The oldest and the most common domestic light source is the tungsten filament incandescent lamp.

2 Clear candle
These slender, candle-shaped lamps have a clear envelope and visible filaments that emulate the brilliance of candlelight.

3 Opaque GLS
Brighly colored incandescent lamps can be used to create theatrical and dramatic lighting effects.

4 Pygmy
Pygmy bulbs are used in a number of different domestic applications, such as exhaust fan hoods, ovens, and refrigerators.

5 Decorative candle
Shaped candles such as this one are designed to be used without a shade in chandeliers and wall sconces.

6 Silvered-bowl GLS
The simplest type of incandescent reflector, silvered-bowl bulbs reflect light back into specially designed fixtures such as a parabolic reflector. Alternatively, they can be used in pendant fixtures to prevent glare.

7 Globe
Opal white globe bulbs emit a soft diffused light that reduces glare and does not cast hard shadows.

8 PAR economy

Parabolic aluminized reflector lamps have a robust front of toughened glass, which enables them to withstand extremes in temperature. They are available as either incandescent or halogen.

9 Spot reflector

A "spot" is a reflector that emits a beam of light that is less than 30 degrees wide.

10 Flood reflector

A "flood" is a reflector that emits a beam greater than 30 degrees wide.

Halogen lamps

In halogen lamps, the filament burns at much higher temperatures than in an incandescent lamp, so the envelope is smaller and made of quartz to withstand the increased heat. Standard household-current halogen lamps can be used in conventional fixtures, but low-voltage halogen lamps require a transformer to reduce the power.

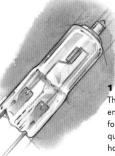

1 Low-voltage capsule

These tiny, compact single-envelope capsules are intended for use with a transformer. The quartz envelope must not be handled with bare hands.

2 Standard household-current halogen

This lamp can be used in household-current fixtures to cast the clear white light characteristic of halogen.

3 Low-voltage halogen dichroic reflector

The dichroic reflector directs light forward and draws heat back, creating a concentrated beam of cool light. It must be used with a transformer.

3 Compact fluorescent globe

This shape recalls the familiar form of a GLS incandescent lamp.

1 Standard tube

The familiar fluorescent "strip light" requires special control gear and is not ideally suited to home use.

Fluorescent lamps

Traditionally, fluorescent lamps have been associated with inhospitable commercial environments. However, recent advances by bulb manufacturers have resulted in new fluorescent lamps that combine the benefits of fluorescent lamps—long life, economy, and energy-efficiency—with the convenience of incandescent.

2 Compact fluorescent tube

These produce a warmer, more welcoming light and have caps that fit household-current fixtures.

Household electrical supplies

Electricity is distributed around the home in a number of different ways, which vary from country to country. In Britain, the most common arrangement usually consists of ring circuits, where the power is routed from the distribution box or consumer unit to a number of sockets around the room and back again to the distribution box. The number of sockets on a ring circuit may be increased by adding "spurs," which extend from individual sockets to provide additional outlets. Each circuit is fused.

In other countries, radial circuits are more common. A radial circuit feeds a number of socket outlets, but, unlike a ring circuit, its cable terminates at the last socket rather than returning to the distribution box.

In addition to a power circuit, houses often have separate lighting circuits, where the wiring is run along the space between the ceiling of one level and the floor of the next, taking power to ceiling-mounted fixtures that are controlled by wall-mounted switches. Household lighting circuits are of the radial type; and take a smaller load than power circuits. In the average house, it is practical to have two separate lighting circuits running from the consumer unit or distribution box, one for the ground floor and another for the upstairs floor.

Electricity is measured in different ways. Wattage is the rate at which electricity is consumed; the higher the wattage, the more powerful the electrical appliance or light source. The wattages of lamps of different light sources are not directly equivalent, however, if you want to compare the amount of light that is actually produced. While a 100-watt incandescent bulb will produce more light than a 25-watt incandescent bulb, for example, a 9-watt compact fluorescent lamp will emit as much light as 40-watt incandescent bulb. Comparisons are usually given on the packaging of low-energy sources to enable you to assess the correct wattage to choose. Light fixtures are generally labeled with the maximum wattage bulb that should be used. This should never be exceeded, or there will be a risk of the fixture overheating or the shade catching fire.

Amperage measures the speed at which the electrical current flows. A higher number of amps indicates a faster, stronger flow.

Volts measure the pressure of electricity. Household current in the United States is 120 volts, while in Britain it is 240 volts, and in Europe it is 220 volts, which is why we need to use an adaptor for our electrical appliances when we travel abroad. Low-voltage lighting (such as low-voltage tungsten halogen) requires a transformer to reduce the power, generally to 12 volts.

The basic electrical installation in a house may need to be upgraded or altered for a number of reasons. The age of the wiring is a critical factor. Wiring that is over twenty years old will probably need to be replaced. Fuses that repeatedly blow can be an indication of a serious fault in the system and therefore should always be investigated by an electrician. More electricity sockets may be required if you wish to increase the number of lamps or appliances running on a circuit and, if the load increases dramatically, you may even need to install an extra circuit. And for a fully controllable lighting installation, you may need different circuits for different groups of lights, each switched separately.

All these alterations require the services of a professional electrician. Indeed, all electrical work, from full-scale rewiring right down to installing a stationary light, should be carried out by a professional electrician in accordance with local regulations. For a full discussion of safety matters, turn to page 182.

An electrician must always be chosen and briefed with care, whether you are planning a major overhaul of your electrical infrastructure or simply intending to install a downlight. There are many hazards associated with faulty lighting or electrical supply. It only takes one incorrectly wired plug to start a fire: in electrical work, unlike other building and service trades, the margin of error is virtually nil. Make sure the electrician you choose is a member of an officially recognized professional association (for details of

recognized bodies see page 187). For very complex lighting arrangements, it may be a good idea to consult a professional lighting designer. Many large retail outlets or lighting specialists provide a design service that can help you to plan and implement a lighting plan for your home. Some even have in-store lighting setups to demonstrate the different effects that can be achieved.

Outdoor installations

There are two main types of outdoor electrical installations: standard household-current voltage and low voltage. A combination of the two systems is also possible. All outdoor electrical installations are strictly work for the professionals. They can be expensive, since they require both specialized fixtures and cabling. Very large outdoor systems may require a separate connection to the main supply via a distribution box; this may also be required if you are using power for other means, to heat a greenhouse, for example.

In household-current systems, power to outdoor installations is routed to weatherproof fixtures via special heavy-duty cabling, which must be buried in conduits in the ground at a depth of no less than 18 inches—deeper still if the cable has to pass under any areas in the garden where digging is likely to take place, such as an herbaceous border.

In low-voltage systems, a transformer is required to reduce the power, and there are regulations governing its positioning so the transformer is protected from the elements while remaining ventilated. The rating of the transformer indicates how many fixtures can be used: a 100-watt transformer, for example, will serve four 25-watt fixtures. Alternatively, fixtures with integral transformers can be chosen. The cabling that runs from transformers to fixtures must be heatproof, but it need not be buried since it carries only a low voltage. As with household-current systems, all low-voltage outdoor fixtures must be weatherproof. Outdoor sockets must always be weatherproof and covered.

Lighting controls

The most basic form of lighting control is the switch. Stationary lights, such as downlights, wall lights, and pendants are controlled by wall switches. Freestanding lights, such as floor and table lamps and task lights, are controlled directly by switches on the fixture itself. Lighting controls such as dimmers allow you to vary light levels according to mood and need. Other types are useful in situations where remote or programmed control is advisable—to deter intruders, for example.

Switches

For electricity to work, there must be a complete circuit for the current to flow through. A open switch is an interruption in the flow; close the switch and the circuit is complete. In the same way, plugging a light into a switched socket connects it with the power supply and allows the electricity to work; in this case, to produce light. There are a wide variety of different types of switches that offer a number of practical advantages as well as a choice of stylistic options.

The standard wall switch is a rocker set into a plastic switch plate. Where there are several circuits, each one controlling a set of lights, multiple switching is a practical format, grouping all the controls for a room in one sensible location—near a door, for example.

In certain locations it can be advisable to substitute switches in which the entire face plate rocks. These switches are extremely easy to operate and can even be flicked by pressure from an elbow. For people who have reduced manual dexterity or for use in areas such as kitchens where the hands may be either full or wet, these switches make a practical alternative.

Standard switches are perfectly adequate, but they contribute little to the aesthetics of a room. For those who care about detail and can afford to spend a little more, changing the switches will enhance the overall look. Stylistic variations range from retro or traditional models to the sleek and contemporary. For a traditional look, choose reproduction wood and brass toggle switches, brass wall plates, or those simulating the old Bakelite finish. Modern designs include see-through acrylic plates or elegant, understated plates made of brushed steel.

Integral switches control a light directly. These vary from the common turn or push variety fitted directly to the bulbholder to switches mounted on the cord or in the form of a foot-controlled floor button. In the United States some direct switches include a "dimmer" option as well as the standard on/off. It is also more common for table lamps to be controlled both individually and by a centrally wired wall switch, so a group of table lamps can be switched off and on at the entrance to the room rather than individually.

Dimmers

There are very few lighting arrangements that would not benefit from the addition of dimming controls. A dimmer reduces the amount of light simply by reducing the power to the light source. In living rooms, bedrooms, bathrooms, and workrooms, dimmers allow fine adjustments to be made to the overall balance of natural, background, and task lighting. Enhancing atmosphere for relaxation is a prime advantage, but by reducing the amount of power that is used, dimmers significantly extend the life of all filament lamps. Not all light sources can be dimmed. Mini or compact fluorescent lights cannot be readily dimmed, nor can some low-voltage lights. All standard incandescent and tungsten halogen lamps can be dimmed.

Dimmer switches come with a wattage rating that governs how many lights they can control. This rating is generally on the low side and means that it is usually only possible to control a couple of lights with one switch, normally the ambient or background lighting. If there is more than one lighting circuit, controlling each different circuit with a dimmer provides maximum versatility.

Dimmers often incorporate an on-off switch. Rotary designs are most common, but there are also sliding and touch-plate controls. Standard dimmers have a tendency to emit a faint humming sound, however, so you may wish to position such controls outside the room. There are also highly sophisticated electronic lighting control systems that incorporate digital displays, individual switches for different circuits, and dimmers in one high-tech panel.

Automatic switches

There are a variety of automatic switches available, some designed to save frustration, some for economical use of light and power, and others to provide security. The simplest form of automatic switch is the type commonly installed on refrigerators, which turns a light on when a door is opened and off when it is closed. These switches are easy to install and make good practical sense for hall closets and other storage areas where light is needed only momentarily.

Timers and time switches can be set in a similar way to a central heating thermostat, to turn lights off and on at specific intervals and give the impression of occupancy. The simplest types plug into a wall socket.

Approach lights can be triggered by heat or motion and are a proven deterrent for intruders, who prefer to operate under cover of darkness. More sophisticated controls are also available in the form of trip switches in which an infrared beam is interrupted, activating lights on the outside or even on the inside of a house.

With increasing computerization, homes of the future may have fully integrated and programmable servicing, with lighting preset to switch on or off at required times, to respond via photosensitive cells to alterations in natural light levels or to the approach of a potential user. The result will be both a highly flexible ambience, and an efficient and economical use of energy. Much of this technology has already been developed, and similar systems are in use in theaters and in large commercial and public spaces. In the smart house of the future, intelligent light may provide a seamless backdrop to living, and switching may be as archaic as striking a match.

Safety and Maintenance

Electricity is potentially lethal, and artificial lighting is one of the most common ways in which we make everyday use of this powerful force. Flicking a switch, plugging in a lamp, or changing a bulb are normal household routines that cause barely a thought, but they bring us into close contact with a source of energy that, under the wrong circumstances, can kill.

The potential hazards associated with lighting and electrical supply are many. Faulty wiring or plugs, overloaded sockets, fraying cords, and overheated fixtures can all cause electric shock or fire. Trailing wires can cause serious falls. Hot bulbs and fixtures can burn. Contact with water or extremes of temperature can cause bulbs to shatter.

For these reasons, and many more, both the installation of wiring and light fixtures is subject to stringent regulations. These vary from country to country; in some parts of the world, such as Germany and Australia, it is illegal for any amateur to carry out even the most minor electrical work. It is strongly advisable to err on the side of safety and always use a reputable professional electrician for any alterations to the lighting or power supply. Turn to page 187 for details of recognized electrical bodies who will be able to recommend an electrician in your area.

This checklist provides a guide to safety and maintenance. Never underestimate the power or danger of electricity. Don't be tempted to cut corners or do without specialized advice.

General

- Choose fixtures from a reputable outlet. If you buy a secondhand or antique light, have it checked by an electrician to make sure it is safe to use.

- Never fit a bulb of a higher wattage than that recommended for a particular fixture.

- Never change bulbs when your hands are wet.

- Allow bulbs to cool down before handling.

- Never handle halogen capsule lamps with bare hands, as the grease from your skin can affect the quartz envelope.

- Old wiring should be checked by a professional and may need to be replaced. Fuses that blow constantly may indicate trouble and should be investigated by a qualified electrician.

- Replace any fraying cords and broken bulbholders.

- Make sure plugs are correctly wired.

- Never overload a power socket or a transformer.

- Avoid trailing cords across the floor, as they may cause accidental tumbles.

- Make sure power is switched off at the junction box before attempting to make any electrical alterations.

- Do not position lights too close to flammable materials, such as paper, fabric, or wood.

Recessed lighting

- Follow manufacturers' guidelines for installation and make sure there is enough ceiling space to provide adequate ventilation.

- Choose fixtures with heat-protective shields.

- Avoid using recessed lighting in old houses where the ceiling space may be cramped or where there may be a buildup of dust and debris in the cavity.

- Make sure access is easy so that lights can be maintained and bulbs changed without undue difficulty.

Halls and stairs

- Light staircases evenly and informatively to avoid both glare and obscuring shadows.

- Avoid trailing cords on stairs and in hallways.

- Position switches near main doors and on landings.

Kitchens

- Illuminate work surfaces fully with even, glare-free light.

- Avoid freestanding fixtures and trailing cords across floors or counters.

- Angle lights carefully to avoid dangerous glare near the stove or work surface.

- Do not overload sockets with lights and appliances.

- Position lights where they will not be splashed with water.

Children's rooms

- Use childproof safety covers on sockets.

- Avoid freestanding floor lamps that can be pulled over by their cords.

- If you wish to use a table lamp, make sure it is sturdy.

- Avoid trailing or dangling cords that might tempt children to tug them.

- Position novelty or decorative fixtures well out of reach.

Bathrooms

- Follow safety regulations to make sure water and electricity do not come into contact with each other. Fixtures should be positioned at least 8 feet away from showers, bathtubs, or sinks unless metallic parts and bulbs are completely enclosed.

- Avoid adjustable lights that you may be tempted to touch with wet hands.

- Avoid pendant lights or any fixtures that leave the bare bulb exposed to splashes.

- Install appropriate sockets and switches. Do not use lights with cords.

Outdoors

- Employ a professional to install outdoor lighting installations.

- Make sure all outdoor fittings are weatherproof; or fully waterproof if they are to be used in ponds or other water features.

- Bury cabling in conduits or make sure it is routed well away from areas where you will be using lawnmowers or other tools.

- Keep fixtures free from leaves and dirt.

- Avoid positioning lights so they dazzle pedestrians or drivers.

Directory of suppliers

LAMPS AND LIGHTING FIXTURES

Most of the suppliers listed below will be able to provide both interior and exterior lighting fixtures.

Altamira Lighting
79 Joyce Street
Warren, RI 02885
401-245-7676
www.altamiralighting.com
Contemporary table and floor lamps, as well as porcelain bottle lamps.

American Period Lighting, Inc.
3004 Columbia Avenue
Lancaster, PA 17603
717-392-5649
www.americanperiod.com
Representations of fixtures that were created 75 to 150 years ago. Custom fixtures and repair work are also available.

Authentic Designs
69 The Mill Road
West Rupert, VT 05776
802-394-7713
http://authentic-designs.com
Handcrafted chandeliers and sconces of solid brass and Vermont maple. They are available electrified or with candles.

Baldinger Architectural Lighting, Inc.
19-02 Steinway Street
Astoria, NY 11105
718-204-5700
www.baldinger.com
Famous-architect-designed fixtures.

Baldwin Brass
841 East Wyomissing Boulevard
Box 15048
Reading, PA 19612
800-566-1986
www.baldwinhardware.com
Classic designs in brass.

The Basic Source, Inc.
655 Carlson Court
Rohnert Park, CA 94928
707-586-5483
www.basicsourcelighting.com
Contract-quality lighting fixtures.

Bed, Bath & Beyond
800-462-3966
Visit www.bedbathandbeyond.com to find a store near you.
Everything for the home, including a wide range of lighting solutions.

The Brass Light Gallery
131 South First Street
Milwaukee, WI 53204
800-243-9595
www.brasslight.com
Lighting from the Arts and Crafts, Mission, and Prairie periods are reproduced from original designs.

Casella Lamps
111 Rhode Island Street
San Francisco, CA 94103
415-626-9600
www.casellalighting.com
Custom-manufactured high-end brass swing-arm and floor lamps.

Frederick Cooper Lamp Co., Inc.
2545 West Diversey Avenue
Chicago, IL 60647
773-384-0800
www.frederickcooper.com
Handsomely designed and finished lamps of all types and styles.

Crate & Barrel
800-967-6696
Visit www.crateandbarrel.com for a store near you.
Furniture, accessories, and lighting.

Electrics Lighting and Design
530 West Francisco Blvd.
San Rafael, CA 94901
415-258-9996
www.electrics.com
Over 100 lighting lines, most from Italy. The emphasis is on modern looks.

Estiluz Inc., USA
235 Moonachie Road
Moonachie, NJ 07074
201-641-1977
www.estiluz.com
Pure and simple designs in a classic transitional style.

Ethan Allen
800-228-9229
Visit www.ethanallen.com for a store near you.
Furniture and lighting for the home.

Häfele America Company
3901 Cheyenne Drive
P.O. Box 4000
Archdale, NC 27263
800-423-3531
www.hafeleonline.com
Low-voltage fixtures for under-cabinet and recessed lighting. Systems are available in both fluorescent and halogen and may be built in or added on.

Hinson & Co.
979 Third Avenue
New York, NY 10022
212-688-7754
Traditional and contemporary table, wall, and floor lamps, as well as the Mrs. MacDougall line of antique reproductions.

IKEA
800-434-4532
Visit www.ikea.com for a store near you.
Furniture and lighting solutions.

Illuminating Experiences
233 Cleveland Avenue
Highland Park, NJ 08904
800-734-5858
Italian and Spanish lighting in contemporary and classic looks.

Juno Lighting, Inc.
1300 South Wolf Road
Des Plaines, IL 60017
847-827-9880
www.junolighting.com
Manufacturers of sleek, modern track and recessed lighting for custom installations.

Kichler Lighting Group
7711 East Pleasant Valley Road
P.O. Box 318010
Cleveland, OH 44131
800-875-4216
www.kichler.com
Any type of lighting from traditional through contemporary chandeliers to solar-powered outdoor fixtures.

Leucos USA
11 Mayfield Ave.
P.O. Box 7829
Edison, NJ 08818
732-225-0010
www.leucos.com
Decorative Murano glass lighting.

Lightforms
168 Eighth Avenue
New York, NY 10011
212-255-4664
http://hometown.aol.com/lightformsny/
Custom-made lamps and lampshades with a contemporary look. Open to the public as well as to the trade.

The Lighting Center Ltd.
240 East 59th Street
New York, NY 10022
212-888-8380
www.lightingcenter-ny.com
Recessed and track lighting as well as chandeliers and free-standing lamps.

Lightolier
631 Airport Road
Fall River, MA 02720
508-679-8131
www.lightolier.com
All types of contemporary lighting are available from this company.

Luceplan USA, Inc.
315 Hudson Street
New York, NY 10013
212-989-6265
www.luceplan.com
Award-winning Italian lamps and fixtures.

Lumetta Inc.
69 Aster Street
West Warwick, RI 02893
877-586-3882
www.lumettainc.com
Contemporary lighting.

Ann-Morris Antiques
239 East 60th Street
New York, NY 10022
212-755-3308
Custom and antique lighting with an English country look. To the trade only.

M. S. K. Illumination, Inc.
969 Third Avenue
New York, NY 10022
212-888-6474
www.mskillumination.com
Everything from architectural to desk lights. Custom products also available.

Niedermaier
400 North Oakley Blvd.
Chicago, IL 60612
312-492-9400 x 200
www.niedermaier.com
Dramatic contemporary table and floor lamps. Call and they will ship direct.

NuLite Ltd.
7001 East 57th Place
Commerce City, CO 80022
303-287-9646
A wide variety of lighting solutions.

Period Lighting Fixtures, Inc.
167 River Road
Clarksburg, MA 01247
800-828-6990
www.periodlighting.com
This company reproduces American fixtures from 1620 to 1850.

Pottery Barn
888-226-3537
Visit www.potterybarn.com for a store near you.
Furniture and lighting for the home.

Progress Lighting
P.O. Box 5704
Spartanburg, SC 29304
864-599-6000
www.progresslighting.com
All types of kitchen lighting. Much of their
work is through building contractors.

Rejuvenation Lamp & Fixture Company
2550 NW Nicolai St.
Portland, OR 97201
888-401-1900
www.rejuvenation.com
Over 250 reproductions of period light
fixtures and lamps from the Arts and
Crafts, Victorian, and Neoclassic eras.

Remington Lamp Co.
5000 Paschall Avenue
Philadelphia, PA 19143
215-729-2600
Residential lamps and lighting in a variety
of finishes and styles.

Restoration Hardware
800-762-1005
Visit www.restorationhardware.com for a
store near you.
Fine hardware, lighting, and other
accessories for the home.

St. Louis Antique Lighting Co.
801 North Skinker Boulevard
St. Louis, MO 63130
314-863-1414
www.traditional-building.com
Custom designs and fabrications and
exact reproductions of fixtures used in
historic buildings. Appraisals are
available.

Joseph Richter, Inc.
249 East 57th Street
New York, NY 10022
212-755-6094
Specialists in tole and other custom-
painted fixtures, this company makes
every piece to order. To the trade only.

Paul Sahlin Tiffany's
1326 Obispo Avenue
Long Beach, CA 90804
800-521-3996
www.pstlamps.com
Stained-glass and antique reproduction
table, ceiling, and floor lamps.

Sirmos
979 Third Avenue 1634
New York, NY 10022
212-371-0910
www.sirmos.com
Hand-cast resin decorative lighting. Each
piece is hand-finished to your
specifications.

Target
Visit www.target.com for a store near you.
One of America's largest retail chains,
featuring a large lighting department.

The Tin Bin
20 Valley Road
Neffsville, PA 17601
717-569-6210
www.thetinbin.com
Modern reproductions with the patina of
antiques. Lamps are available for indoors
and outdoor use, electrified or candle.

Top Brass Lighting
3502 Parkdale Avenue
Baltimore, MD 21211
800-359-4135
Unique lamps and lighting, including a
range of interesting sconces, in styles that
range from antique to contemporary.

Urban Archaeology
143 Franklin Street
New York, NY 10013
212-431-4646
www.urbanarchaeology.com
Indoor and outdoor lighting fixtures made
in brass and other metals.

W.A.C Lighting
615 South Street
Garden City, NY 11530
800-526-2588
www.waclighting.com
Discreet and subtle track and recessed
lighting.

OUTDOOR LIGHTING

The Copper House
1747 Dover Road
Route 4
Epsom, NH 03234
800-281-9798
www.thecopperhouse.com
Early American fixtures.

Heritage Lanterns
25 Yarmouth Crossing Drive
Yarmouth, ME 04096
800-648-4449
www.heritagelanterns.com
Reproduction fixtures.

Washington Copper Works
49 South Street
Washington, CT 06793
860-868-7527
www.washingtoncopperworks.com
Meticulous reproductions of classic
American fixtures in a variety of finishes.

CHANDELIERS

ABC Carpet & Home
888 Broadway
New York, NY 10003
212-473-3000
www.abchome.com
Over 1,000 antique and reproduction
lighting fixtures from all over the world.

Arte de Mexico
1000 Chestnut Street
Burbank, CA 91506
818-753-4559
www.artedemexico.com
More than 300 unique styles and 21 hand-
applied finishes.

Greene's Lighting
1059 Third Avenue
New York, NY 10021
212-753-2507
Custom-made chandeliers.

Louis Lamps
7332 Frankford Avenue
Philadelphia, PA 19136
215-338-2978
Ornate, hand-cut crystal chandeliers and
candelabras. Replacements parts are also
available.

Original Cast Lighting Co.
6120 Delmar Boulevard
St. Louis, MO 63112
314-863-1895
www.theocl.com
Art Deco-inspired chandeliers, ceiling
fixtures, and sconces.

Schonbek Worldwide Lighting, Inc.
800-836-1892
www.schonbek.com
America's largest manufacturer of crystal
chandeliers, with innovative contemporary
and traditional designs.

Waterford Crystal
800-677-7860
Visit www.waterford.com for a store near
you.
Cut-crystal chandeliers, sconces, and
hurricanes.

SPECIALTY LIGHTING

Aladdin Mantle Lamp Company
681 International Blvd.
Clarksville, TN 37040
800-457-5267
www.aladdinlamps.com
Well-designed oil and kerosene lamps.
Factory reconstructions of their antique
lamps are sold through antique shops.

Barry of Chelsea Antiques
154 Ninth Avenue
New York, NY 10011
212-242-2666
Victorian and turn-of-century glass-shaded
lighting.

L.L. Bean
Freeport, ME 04033
800-441-5713
Camping hotline: 800-226-7552
www.llbean.com
Outdoor lighting, from candle lanterns
to propane lanterns can be found in
L. L. Bean's special sporting catalog.

Campbell Lamp Supply
1108 Pottstown Pike
West Chester, PA 19380
610-696-8070
Everything you need to complete or adapt
an antique oil lamp.

City Lights
2226 Massachusetts Avenue
Cambridge, MA 02140
617-547-1490
www.citylights.nu
Antique lighting from 1850 to 1950; call to
explain what you want and they will send
photos of what they have available.

Coleman Co., Inc.
Box 2931
Wichita, KS 67201
800-835-3278
www.coleman.com
Gas-powered lanterns that use propane,
unleaded gas, and Coleman Fuel.

Conant Custom Brass, Inc.
270 Pine Street
Burlington, VT 05401
800-832-4484
www.conantcustombrass.com
Services include metal polishing,
lacquering, and gold leafing. They can also
handle custom fabrication.

Hunter Fan Company
800-448-6837
Visit www.hunterfan.com for a retailer
near you.
Silent ceiling fans with built-in lighting.

Knoll
1235 Water Street
East Greenville, PA 18041
800-343-5665
www.knoll.com
Modern and ergonomic desk lamps from
original designers.

Lava World International, Inc.
A division of Haggerty Enterprises, Inc.
430 Kimberly Drive
Carol Stream, IL 60188
630-315-3300
www.lavaworld.com
Originators of the funky Lava lamp.

Mobilier
180 Franklin Street
New York, NY 10013
212-334-6197
Vintage French furnishings from the 1940s
and '50s, including an interesting array of
lighting fixtures and lamps.

Roy Electric Co., Inc.
22 Elm Street
Westfield, NJ 07090
800-366-3347
www.royelectric.com
Victorian and turn-of-the-century
reproduction lighting fixtures.

LAMPSHADES

When shopping for a new shade, bring your lamp with you to assure a perfect match.

Just Shades, Inc.
21 Spring Street
New York, NY 10002
212-966-2757
Lampshades in a number of styles.
Custom work is available.

Hollywood Lights Shades
A division of Wisconsin Lighting, Inc.
800 Wisconsin Street
Suite D02-104
Eau Claire, WI 54703
800-657-6999
www.wilighting.com
Self-adhesive shades that can be made up in your own fabric or wallcovering.
Available in craft stores.

Mainely Shades
100 Gray Road
Falmouth, ME 04105
207-797-7568
www.mainelyshades.com
Everything you need to enable you to make your own lampshades.

Shady Lady
5020 West Eisenhower
Loveland, CO 80537
970-699-1080
www.shadyladylampshades.com
Fine fabric shades especially suited to Victorian lamp styles.

CANDLES

Carolina Candle Supplies
8421 Old Statesville Road #2
Charlotte, NC 28269
704-599-1225
www.carolinacandlesupplies.com
Tapers, votives, tea lights, and pillars, scented and unscented.

Colonial Candles of Cape Cod
232 Main Street
Hyannis, MA 02601
Mail orders: 800-437-1238
www.colonialathome.com
Pillars, hand-dipped tapers, and classic candles in a wide range of colors.

Covington Candle
976 Lexington Avenue #A
New York, NY 10021
212-472-1131
Tapers in 30 colors and six sizes. Pillars available in various sizes and to order.

Creative Candles
P.O. Box 412514
Kansas City, MO 64141
816-474-9711
www.creativecandles.com
Tapers, pillars, and spheres in 44 colors.

Illuminations
800-226-3537
www.illuminations.com
76 stores nationwide carry a wide selection of hand-crafted candles.

Northern Lights Candles
3474 Andover Road
Wellsville, NY 14895
585-593-1200
www.northernlightscandles.com
Candles of all varieties are available here, from scented to molded novelty shapes.

Yankee Candle Company
800-243-1776
www.yankeecandle.com
The leading designer, manufacturer, retailer and wholesaler of premium scented candles in the U.S.

LIGHTING CONSULTANTS

These consultants all do custom work. Talk to them about what you want done and they'll provide an estimate or beg off if the job is too small.

Bouyea & Associates, Inc.
5 Greenhill Road
Washington Depot, CT 06794
214-520-6580
Contact: Barbara Bouyea

H.M. Brandston & Partners, Inc.
122 West 26th Street
5th Floor
New York, NY 10001
212-924-4050
www.hmbp.com

Randy Burkett Lighting Design, Inc.
609 East Lockwood Ave.
Suite 201
St. Louis, MO 63119
314-961-6650
www.rbldi.com

Edward J. Cansino Lighting Design
1620 School Street
Suite 102
Moraga, CA 94556
925-376-9497
www.ejc.com

Cline Bettridge Bernstein Lighting Design
30 West 22nd Street
New York, NY 10010
212-741-3280
www.cbbld.com
Contact: Stephen Bernstein

Ross De Alessi Lighting Design
3313 West McGraw St.
Seattle, WA 98199
206-441-0870
www.dealessi.com

Francis Krahe & Associates
304 South Broadway
Suite 500
Los Angeles, CA 90013
213-617-0477
www.fkaild.com

Lighting and Design Consultants
555 South Palm Canyon Drive
Palm Springs, CA 92264
760-320-5599
Contact: James Callahan

Lighting Design Alliance
1234 East Burnett Street
Signal Hill, CA 90755
562-989-3843
www.lightingdesignalliance.com
Contact: Charles Israel

Luminae Souter Lighting Design
504 Roosevelt Way
San Francisco, CA 94114
415-865-8800
www.luminae-souter.com
Contact: Michael Souter

Patrick B. Quigley & Associates, Inc.
2340 Plaza Del Amo
Suite 125
Torrance, CA 90501
310-533-6064
www.pbqa.com

Rising Sun Enterprises, Inc.
40 Sunset Drive #1
Basalt, CO 81621
970-927-8051
www.selight.com

Spectrum Lighting Design
175 South Main Street
Suite 300
Salt Lake City, UT 84111
800-678-7077
www.spectrum-engineers.com/spectrumlighting.html
Contact: Glenn Johnson

Wigmore Lighting Designs
70 Washington Street
Suite 509
Brooklyn, NY 11201
718-222-4108
www.johnwigmore.com

Yarnell Associates
5030 Mackey St.
Suite 100
Overland Park, KS 66203
913-384-2801
www.yarnellassociates.com

ASSOCIATIONS

The American Lighting Association
P.O. Box 420288
Dallas, TX 75342
800-274-4484
www.theamericanlightingassoc.com
Call the 800 number for details of three members' showrooms in your local area.

International Association of Lighting Designers
Merchandise Mart
Suite 9-104
200 World Trade Center
Chicago, IL 60654
312-527-3677
www.iald.org
The lighting consultants listed above are all members of this organization who work in the residential area.

Architects and designers whose work is featured in this book

Alidad
The Lighthouse
Gasworks
2 Michael Road
London SW6 2AD
page 28 left

Ann Boyd Design Ltd
33 Elystan Place
London SW3 3NT
page 86

Asfour Guzy Architects
594 Broadway
New York NY 10012
212-334-9350
easfour@asfourguzy.com
page 110 above

Ash Sakula Architects
24 Rosebery Avenue
London EC1R 4SX
+44 20 7837 9735
www.ashsak.com
page 138

Bilhuber Inc.
330 East 59th Street
6th Floor
New York, NY 10022
212-308-4888
pages 14 below, 50 left and centre, 72 centre, 73, 116 above right, 119, 133, 155

Brookes Stacey Randall
16 Winchester Walk
London SE1 9AQ
+44 20 7403 0707
www.bsr-architects.com
pages 25, 60 above, 63, 136–137, 146–147, 153 centre

Bruce Bierman Design, Inc.
29 West 15 Street
New York, NY 10011
212-243-1935
www.biermandesign.com
page 27

Tito Canella (Canella & Achilli
Architects) Milan
Via Revere # 7/9
20123 Milan
Italy
+39 02 469 5222
www.canella-achilli.com
page 1

Chester Jones Ltd
Interior Designers
240 Battersea Park Road
London SW11 4NG
+44 20 7498 2717
chester.jones@virgin.net
page 43 right

Circus Architects
Unit 111 The Foundry
165 Blackfriars Road
London SE1 8EN
+44 20 7953 7322
*pages 22 left, 29, 34–35, 74, 86,
116 above left, 117, 143 below, 151
152, 153 right*

Damien D'Arcy Associates
9 Lamington Street
London W6 0HU
+44 20 8741 1193
pages 56 above right, 114–115

Dive Architects
10 Park Street
London SE1 9AB
+44 20 7407 0955
www.divearchitects.com
pages 60–61

Ory Gomez
Didier Gomez
15 rue Henri Heine
75016 Paris
France
+33 01 44 30 88 23
orygomez@free.fr
page 2

Gustavo Martinez Design
206 Fifth Avenue, 4th Floor
New York, NY 10010
212-686-3102
gmdecor@aol.com
page 90 below

IPL Interiors
25 Bullen Street
Battersea
London SW11 3ER
+44 20 7978 4224
*pages 20 below right, 52 left, 53 above
left, 56 above, 91 below, 114–115, 137, 154*

Jennifer Post Design Inc.
Spatial & Interior Designer
25 East 67th Street, 8D
New York, NY 10021
212-734-7994
jpostdesign@aol.com
pages 80 below right, 81

Johnson Schwinghammer
335 West 38th Street # 9
New York, NY 10018
212-643-1552
www.jslighting.com
pages 16–17, 26, 75 left

Laura Bohn Design Associates
30 West 26th Street
New York, NY 10010
212-645-3636
www.laurabohndesign.com
pages 30, 38, 46–47, 57

McDowell+Benedetti
Architects
68 Rosebery Avenue
London EC1R 4RR
+44 20 7278 8810
email@McDowellBenedetti.com
Page 30 above

Fatto A Mano
by Lucretia Moroni Ltd
127 Madison Avenue
4th Floor
New York, NY 10016
212-686-4848
pages 28, 50 right, 53 above right

Mark Guard Architects
161 Whitfield Street
London W1P 5RY
+44 20 7380 1199
*pages 10–11, 13, 16, 41, 54–55, 59,
76 above*

Amanda Martocchio, Architect
189 Brushy Ridge Road
New Canaan, CT 06840
page 90 below

Clare Mosley
Gilding, eglomisé panels & mirrors,
lampbases, finials & curtain accessories
+44 20 7708 3123
page 94

Mullman Seidman Architects
Architecture & Interior Design
443 Greenwich Street, # 2A
New York, NY 10013
212-431-0770
msa@mullmanseidman.com
page 80 above right

Myra Hoefer Design
243 Center Street
Healdsburg, CA 95448
707-433-7837
pages 48, 52 above right, 90 above

Reed Creative Services Ltd
151a Sydney Street
London SW3 6NT
+44 20 7565 0066
pages 2, 22 right, 106–107, 113, 135

Nico Rensch Architeam
www.architeam.co.uk
*pages 71, 75 right, 112, 144 below left,
150 above, 157 below*

Retrouvius Reclamation & Design
2a Ravensworth Road
London NW10 5NR
+44 20 8960 6060
www.retrouvius.com
page 156 below

Sergisson Bates
44 Newman Street
London W1P 3PA
+44 20 7255 1564
pages 49, 58–59, 136 below

Shelton, Mindel & Associates
216 18th Street
New York, NY 10011
212-243-3939
*pages 16–17, 26, 68, 75 left, 83 right, 94,
126–127, 158–159*

Site Specific Ltd
60 Peartree Street
London EC1V 3SB
+44 20 7490 3176
www.sitespecificltd.co.uk
page 157 above

Seth Stein, Architect
15 Grand Union Centre
West Row
London W10 5AS
+44 20 8968 8581
*pages 8–9, 12, 18, 31, 32–33, 56–57, 60
below, 76–77, 84–85, 124–125*

Sally Storey
John Cullen Lighting
585 King's Road
London SW6 2EH
+44 20 7371 5400
*pages 106–107, 123 below, 135,
138–139, 143 above*

Studio Works
6775 Centinela Avenue
Building # 3
Culver City, CA 90230
301-390-5051
pages 20 left, 60–61, 153 left

Urban Salon Ltd
Architects
Unit D
Flat Iron Yard
Ayres Street
London SE1 1ES
+44 20 7357 8800
page 42, 72 centre

USE Architects
Unit 12
47–49 Tudor Road
London E9 7SN
+44 20 8986 8111
www.usearchitects.com
page 76br

Vicente Wolf Associates Inc.
333 West 39th Street
New York, NY 10018
212-465-0590
www.vicentewolfassociates.com
*pages 15, 28–29, 77, 78 below, 110 below
right, 132–133*

Vivien Lawrence Interior Design
Interior designer of private homes – any
project from start to finish, small or large.
London
+44 20 8209 0058/+44 20 8209 0562
vl-interiordesign@cwcom.net
page 92 left

Constanze von Unruh
Constanze Interior Projects
Interior Design Company
Richmond, Surrey
+44 20 8948 5533
constanze@constanzeinteriorprojects.com
page 20 left

Daniela Micol Wajskol
Interior Designer
Via Vincenzo Monti 42
20123 Milano
Italy
daniela.w@tiscalinet.it
page 118, 156 above

Wallensteen & Co ab
Architect and Design Consultants
Floragatan 11
114 31 Stockholm
Sweden
46 8 210151
wallensteen@chello.se
Lighting: Konkret Architects/Gerhard Rehm
page 92–93

Greg Yale Landscape Illumination
27 Henry Road
Southampton
New York, NY 11968
516-287-2312
*pages 36–37, 51, 52 above left and below,
91 above, 164 below, 165 above left*

Yeoward South
The Old Imperial Laundry
71 Warriner Gardens
London SW11 4XW
+44 20 7498 4811
wy@yeowardsouth.com
page 131

Picture Credits

All pictures by Ray Main unless specified below:

1 ph Chris Everard/An apartment in Milan designed by Tito Canella of Canella & Achilli Architects; 2 ph Jan Baldwin/Interior Designer Didier Gomez's apartment in Paris; 3 an apartment in New York designed by Laura Bohn Design Associates Inc., lighting from Lightforms; 4-5 lighting by Babylon Design; 6 lighting from William Yeoward; 7 top row left lighting by SKK; 7 top row center left Greg Yale's house in Southampton, NY; 7 top row center right lighting by Fulham Kitchens; 7 top row right Greg Yale's house in Southampton, NY; 7 second row center left Julie Prisca's house in Normandy; 7 second row right light by Tsé Tsé associées, Catherine Levy and Sigolène Prébois; 7 third row left Julie Prisca's house in Normandy; 7 third row center left light from Habitat; 7 third row center right light by Tom Kirk from Space; 7 third row right lighting by SKK; 7 bottom row left light from Ingo Maurer from London Lighting; 7 bottom row center left lighting by SKK; 7 bottom row right light by Tsé Tsé associées, Catherine Levy and Sigolène Prébois; 8-9 a house in London designed by Seth Stein and Sarah Delaney; 10-11 a house in London designed by Mark Guard Architects; 12 Seth Stein's house in London; 13 a house in London designed by Mark Guard Architects; 14 above ph Polly Wreford; 14 below ph David Brittain; 15 ph Chris Everard/Jonathan Wilson's apartment in London, light courtesy of SCP; 16 a house in London designed by Mark Guard Architects; 16-17 Lee F. Mindel's apartment in New York designed by Shelton Mindel & Associates with Associate Architect Reed Morrison, lighting designed by Johnson Schwinghammer and available from Bega, MSK Illuminations; 18 a house in London designed by Seth Stein and Sarah Delaney; 19 Nello Renault's loft in Paris; 20 left ph Jan Baldwin/Constanze von Unruh's house in London; 20 center right Mark Jenning's apartment in New York designed by Asfour Guzy; 20 below right a house in London designed by François Gilles and Dominique Lubar of IPL Interiors; 20-21 Lee F. Mindel's apartment in New York designed by Shelton Mindel & Associates with Associate Architect Reed Morrison; 22 left an apartment in London designed by Circus Architects; 22 right Jonathan Reed's apartment in London, lighting designed by Sally Storey, Design Director of John Cullen Lighting; 22-23 a house in East Hampton, interior by Vicente Wolf; 23 below left Darren and Sheila Chadwick's apartment in London designed by Sergisson Bates; 23 below center Andrea Luria and Zachary Feuer's house in Los Angeles designed by Studio Works, Robert Mangurian and Mary-Ann Ray; 23 below right Gai Harris' apartment in London designed by François Gilles and Dominique Lubar of IPL Interiors; 24 above left a house in London designed by Seth Stein and Sarah Delaney; 24 above right Gai Harris' apartment in London designed by François Gilles and Dominique Lubar of IPL Interiors; 24 below an apartment in London designed by Brookes Stacey Randall; 25 an apartment in London designed by Brookes Stacey Randall; 26 Lee F. Mindel's apartment in New York designed by Shelton, Mindel & Associates with Associate Architect Reed Morrison, lighting designed by Johnson Schwinghammer; 27 ph Chris Everard/Central Park West Residence, New York City designed by Bruce Bierman Design, Inc.; 28 left ph Fritz von der Schulenburg/Alidad's apartment in London; 28-29 a house in East Hampton, interior by Vicente Wolf; 29 right ph Christopher Drake/Valentina Albini's home in Milan; 30 above ph Ray Main/ David & Claudia Dorrell's apartment in London designed in conjunction with McDowell + Benedetti; 30 below an apartment in New York designed by Laura Bohn Design Associates Inc., light from Lightforms; 31 a house in London designed by Seth Stein and Sarah Delaney; 32 Seth Stein's house in London, wall light by Serge Mouille; 33 Seth Stein's house in London, light by Erco; 34-35 an apartment in London designed by Circus Architects; 36 Nello Renault's loft in Paris; 36-37 Greg Yale's house in Southampton, NY; 37 Lee F. Mindel's apartment in New York, lighting designed by Johnson Schwinghammer; 38 an apartment in New York designed by Laura Bohn Design Associates Inc.; 38-39 Nello Renault's loft in Paris; 40 Julie Prisca's house in Normandy; 41 Bryan Hunt and Lucy Kate Asquith's loft in London designed by Mark Guard Architects; 42 ph Chris Everard/Simon Crookall's apartment in London designed by Urban Salon, light courtesy of SCP; 43 left Lee F. Mindel's apartment in New York, lighting designed by Johnson Schwinghammer, light from Mobilier; 43 right ph Jan Baldwin/Designer Chester Jones' house in London; 46-47 an apartment in New York designed by Laura Bohn Design Associates Inc., light from Lightforms; 48 ph James Morris/Skywood House near London designed by Graham Phillips; 49 Darren and Sheila Chadwick's apartment in London designed by Sergisson Bates; 50 left a house in Pennsylvania designed by Jeffrey Bilhuber, light by Hansen Lighting from Hinson & Co; 50 center a house in Pennsylvania designed by Jeffrey Bilhuber, light from Joseph Richter Inc.; 50 right an apartment in New York designed by Lucretia Moroni; 51 Greg Yale's house in Southampton, NY; 52 left ph Christopher Drake/Dominique Lubar for IPL Interiors; 52 above right ph Chris Everard/Jonathan Wilson's apartment in London; 52 below right Greg Yale's house in Southampton, NY; 53 above left Gai Harris' apartment in London designed by François Gilles and Dominique Lubar of IPL Interiors; 53 above right ph Fritz von der Schulenburg/ Irene & Giorgio Silvagni's house in Provence 53 below Greg Yale's house in Southampton, NY; 54-55 Bryan Hunt and Lucy Kate Asquith's loft in London designed by Mark Guard Architects; 56 above Gai Harris' apartment designed by François Gilles and Dominique Lubar of IPL Interiors and Architect Damien D'Arcy Associates; 56 below Malin Iovino's apartment in London; 56-57 Seth Stein's house in London, light by Erco; 57 below an apartment in New York designed by Laura Bohn Design Associates Inc., light from Lightforms; 58-59 Darren and Sheila Chadwick's apartment in London designed by Sergisson Bates; 59 Bryan Hunt and Lucy Kate Asquith's loft in London designed by Mark Guard Architects; 60 above left and right an apartment in London designed by Brookes Stacey Randall; 60 below Seth Stein's house in London; 60-61 ph Debi Treloar/ Family home, Bankside, London; 61 above center Lee F. Mindel's apartment in New York, lighting design by Johnson Schwinghammer; 61 above right Darren and Sheila Chadwick's apartment in London designed by Sergisson Bates; 62 light from Mathmos; 63 an apartment in London designed by Brookes Stacey Randall; 65 lighting by SKK; 68 Lee F. Mindel's apartment in New York designed by Shelton, Mindel & Associates with Associate Architect Reed Morrison; 69 a loft in London designed by Nico Rensch, light from SKK; 70-71 light by Artemide; 71 right a loft in London designed by Nico Rensch, lighting by SKK; 72 left ph Chris Everard/Glenn Carwithen & Sue Miller's house in London, light courtesy of Coexistence; 72 center Chris Everard/Simon Crookall's apartment in London designed by Urban Salon, light courtesy of Geoffrey Drayton; 72 right light by Artemide; 73 a house in Pennsylvania designed by Jeffrey Bilhuber, light from The Lighting Center; 74 a loft in London designed by Circus Architects, ceiling lights from Basis Lighting; 75 left Lee F. Mindel's apartment in New York, designed by Shelton, Mindel & Associates with Associate Architect Reed Morrison, lighting design by Johnson Schwinghammer; 75 right a loft in London designed by Nico Rensch; 76 above a house in London designed by Mark Guard Architects; 76 below left Mark Jennings' apartment in New York designed by Asfour Guzy; 76 below right 76 below right ph Chris Everard/ An apartment in London designed by Jo Hagan of Use Architects; 76-77 a house in London designed by Seth Stein and Sarah Delaney; 77 a house in East Hampton, interior by Vicente Wolf; 78 above light by Erco; 78 below Vicente Wolf's house in Long Island, lighting from Lightforms; 79 above Nello Renault's loft in Paris; 80 above right ph Chris Everard/Suze Orman's apartment in New York designed by Patricia Seidman of Mullman Seidman Architects; 80 below right ph Alan Williams/Stanley & Nancy Grossman's apartment in New York designed by Jennifer Post Design; 81 ph Alan Williams/Jennifer & Geoffrey Symonds' apartment in New York designed by Jennifer Post Design; 82 above left Malin Iovino's apartment in London; 82 above right Adrian Johnston's loft in London, light from Capital Electrical Wholesalers; 82 below a loft in London designed by Nico Rensch; 83 left Adrian Johnston's loft in London, lighting from Capital Electrical Wholesalers; 83 right Lee F. Mindel's apartment in New York, designed by Shelton, Mindel & Associates with Associate Architect Reed Morrison, lighting design by Johnson Schwinghammer; 84-85 Seth Stein's house in London; 85 above left and above right an apartment in New York designed by Laura Bohn Design Associates Inc.; 85 center below Gai Harris' apartment in London designed by François Gilles and Dominique Lubar of IPL Interiors, light from Hector Finch; 85 below a house in London designed

by François Gilles and Dominique Lubar of IPL Interiors, lights covered by Mosaik; 86 ph Chris Everard/Interior Designer Ann Boyd's own apartment in London; 87 left an apartment in London designed by Brookes Stacey Randall, light by Iguzzini; 87 center John Howell's loft in London designed by Circus Architects; 88 above left photograph by James Merrell/Andrew Arnott and Karin Schack's house in Melbourne, Australia; 88 above right light from Hector Finch; 88 center left light from Ann Morris; 88 center right light by Tom Dixon; 88 below left photograph by James Merrell/Andrew Arnott and Karin Schack's house in Melbourne, Australia; 89 ph Alan Williams/Director of design consultants Graven Images, Janice Kirkpatrick's apartment in Glasgow; 90 above Gilles and Cheryle Wicker's apartment in Paris designed by Myra Hoefer Design; 90 below ph Debi Treloar/A family home in Manhattan, designed by architect Amanda Martocchio and Gustavo Martinez Design; 91 above ph Andrew Wood/Norma Holland's house in London; 91 below a house in London designed by François Gilles and Dominique Lubar of IPL Interiors; 92 left ph Christopher Drake/Vivien Lawrence an interior designer in London (020 8209 0562); 92 center light from The Conran Shop; 92 right light from Mathmos; 92-93 ph Andrew Wood/Christer Wallensteen's apartment in Stockholm, Sweden. Lighting: Konkret Architects/Gerhard Rehm; 93 above and below light by Arteluce from Atrium; 93 center light by Charlotte Packe from Space; 93 below light from Atrium; 94 ph Christopher Drake/Clare Mosley's house in London; 95 above left Lee F. Mindel's apartment in New York, light from MSK Illuminations; 95 above center light from Babylon Design; 95 above right a house in East Hampton, interior by Vicente Wolf, light from Niedermaier; 95 below ph Debi Treloar/Catherine Chermayeff & Jonathan David's family home in New York, designed by Asfour Guzy Architects; 96 light from Babylon Design; 97 above left ph Chris Everard/Christina Wilson's house in London, light courtesy of SCP; 97 above right light from Babylon Design; 97 below left light from Atrium; 97 below right an apartment in London designed by Circus Architects; 98 above left a loft in London designed by Nico Rensch; 98 above right light by Artemide; 98 below Lee F. Mindel's apartment in New York, light from Pollock & Associates; 99 above left light by Artemide; 100 left Jonathan Reed's

apartment in London, light by Best & Lloyd; 100 right light from Ecart International; 101 a house in Pennsylvania designed by Jeffrey Bilhuber; 102 above left light by Ingo Maurer from London Lighting; 102 above right lights by Tsé Tsé associées, Catherine Levy and Sigolène Prébois; 102 below ph Debi Treloar/Wim and Josephine's apartment in Amsterdam; 103 above left light from Space; 103 above right light by Tsé Tsé associées, Catherine Levy and Sigolène Prébois; 103 below light by Ingo Maurer from London Lighting; 104-105 Gai Harris' apartment in London designed by François Gilles and Dominique Lubar of IPL Interiors; 106-107 Jonathan Reed's apartment in London, lighting designed by Sally Storey, Design Director of John Cullen Lighting; 108 a house in London designed by Ash Sakula Architects, light from Habitat; 109 light by Hansen Lighting from Hinson & Co; 110 above Mark Jennings' apartment in New York designed by Asfour Guzy; 110 below left a house in London designed by Seth Stein and Sarah Delaney; 110 below right Vicente Wolf's house in Long Island; 111 Nello Renault's loft in Paris; 112 a loft in London designed by Nico Rensch; 113 left Jonathan Reed's apartment in London, lighting designed by Sally Storey, Design Director of John Cullen Lighting; 113 right Jonathan Reed's apartment in London, lights by Best & Lloyd; 114 Julie Prisca's house in Normandy; 114-115 Gai Harris' apartment in London designed by François Gilles and Dominique Lubar of IPL Interiors, Architect Damien D'Arcy Associates, lights from John Cullen Lighting; 116 above left an apartment in London designed by Circus Architects, lights from SKK; 116 above right a house in Pennsylvania designed by Jeffrey Bilhuber; 117 John Howell's loft in London designed by Circus Architects; 118 ph ph Chris Everard/An apartment in Milan designed by Daniela Micol Wajskol, interior designer; 119 a house in Pennsylvania designed by Jeffrey Bilhuber; 120-121 above Lee F. Mindel's apartment in New York, light from MSK Illuminations; 120-121 below a house in East Hampton, interior by Vicente Wolf, light by Hansen Lighting from Hinson & Co; 121 above left Gilles and Cheryle Wicker's apartment in Paris designed by Myra Hoefer Design, light from Mis en Demeure; 121 above right Alex and Charlie Manners' house in London; 121 below left Jonathan Reed's apartment in London, light from William Yeoward; 121 below right a house in London designed by François Gilles and Dominique Lubar of IPL Interiors, light from Besselink & Jones; 122 a house in

East Hampton, interior by Vicente Wolf; 123 above left lights from John Cullen Lighting; 123 below Jonathan Reed's apartment in London, lighting designed by Sally Storey, Design Director of John Cullen Lighting; 123 above center Mark Jennings' apartment in New York designed by Asfour Guzy; 123 above right lighting by John Cullen Lighting; 124-125 Seth Stein's house in London; 126-127 Lee F. Mindel's apartment in New York designed by Shelton, Mindel & Associates with Associate Architect Reed Morrison, lighting design by Johnson Schwinghammer; 128 left Alex and Charlie Manners' house in London, lighting designed by Sally Storey, Design Director of John Cullen Lighting; 128 right Jonathan Reed's apartment in London, lighting designed by Sally Storey, Design Director of John Cullen Lighting; 129 above a house in East Hampton, lighting designed by Vicente Wolf; 129 below a house in Pennsylvania designed by Jeffrey Bilhuber; 130 above left light from Babylon Design; 130 above right a house in Pennsylvania designed by Jeffrey Bilhuber, light by Isamu Noguchi; 130 below light from Mathmos; 131 ph Christopher Drake/William Yeoward & Colin Orchard's home in London; 132-133 Vicente Wolf's house in Long Island, lights designed by Vicente Wolf; 133 a house in Pennsylvania designed by Jeffrey Bilhuber; 134 above Mark Jennings' apartment in New York designed by Asfour Guzy; 134 below a loft in London designed by Nico Rensch; 135 Jonathan Reed's apartment in London, lighting designed by Sally Storey, Design Director of John Cullen Lighting; 136 above a house in London designed by Seth Stein and Sarah Delaney; 136 below Darren and Sheila Chadwick's apartment in London designed by Sergisson Bates; 136-137 an apartment in London designed by Brookes Stacey Randall; 137 Gai Harris' apartment in London designed by François Gilles and Dominique Lubar of IPL Interiors; 138 a house in London designed by Ash Sakula Architects; 138-139 Alex and Charlie Manners' house in London, lighting designed by Sally Storey, Design Director of John Cullen Lighting; 139 a loft in London designed by Circus Architects, light from Fulham Kitchens; 140 above Seth Stein's house in London; 140 below Malin Iovino's apartment in London; 141 Malin Iovino's apartment in London; 142 above Nello Renault's loft in Paris; 142 below Greg Yale's house in Southampton, NY; 143 above Alex and Charlie Manners' house in London, lighting designed by Sally Storey, Design Director of John Cullen Lighting;

143 below an apartment in London designed by Circus Architects; 144 below left a loft in London designed by Nico Rensch, light from SKK; 144 below right Gai Harris' apartment in London designed by François Gilles and Dominique Lubar of IPL Interiors, light from Graham + Greene; 145 Vicente Wolf's house in Long Island, light from Lee Studio; 146-147 an apartment in London designed by Brookes Stacey Randall; 148 above Julie Prisca's house in Normandy; 148-149 Julie Prisca's house in Normandy; 149 above Malin Iovino's apartment in London; 149 below Lee F. Mindel's apartment in New York, lights from Hemisphere; 150 above ph Debi Treloar/A family home in London; 150 below Malin Iovino's apartment in London; 151 ph Debi Treloar/The Boyes' home in London designed by Circus Architects; 152 John Howell's loft in London designed by Circus Architects, lights from Concord; 153 left Andrea Luria and Zachary Feuer's house in Los Angeles designed by Studio Works, Robert Mangurian and Mary-Ann Ray; 153 center an apartment in London designed by Brookes Stacey Randall; 153 right a loft in London designed by Circus Architects; 154 left and center Gai Harris' apartment in London designed by François Gilles and Dominique Lubar of IPL Interiors; 154 right a house in London designed by François Gilles and Dominique Lubar of IPL Interiors; 154-155 a house in East Hampton, interior by Vicente Wolf; 155 left a house in Pennsylvania designed by Jeffrey Bilhuber; 155 center ph Chris Everard/One New Inn Square, a private dining room and home of chef David Vanderhook, all enquiries 020 7729 3645; 155 right a house in Pennsylvania designed by Jeffrey Bilhuber; 156 above ph Chris Everard/An apartment in Milan designed by Daniela Micol Wajskol, interior designer; 156 below ph Chris Everard/Photographer Guy Hills' house in London designed by Joanna Rippon and Maria Speake of Retrouvius; 157 above ph Chris Everard/An actor's London home designed by Site Specific; 157 below a loft in London designed by Nico Rensch; 158-159 Lee F. Mindel's apartment in New York designed by Shelton, Mindel & Associates with Associate Architect Reed Morrison and lighting design by Johnson Schwinghammer; 160 left a house in Pennsylvania designed by Jeffrey Bilhuber; 160 right Seth Stein's house in London; 161 below Vicente Wolf's house in Long Island; 164 below Greg Yale's house in Southampton, NY; 165 above left Greg Yale's house in Southampton, NY.

Index

Publishers' acknowledgments

The publishers would like to thank those architects, designers, and location owners who kindly gave us permission to photograph their work and homes for this book. They would also like to thank the following retailers, who lent us lights to photograph: Artemide UK, Atrium, Babylon Design, London Lighting Co., Mathmos, Purves & Purves, and Space.

Author's acknowledgments

I would like to thank Andy Green for reading the manuscript and making valuable comments and Annabel Morgan, Ashley Western, Ray Main, and Nadine Bazar for all their work in putting the book together so beautifully.